# Proclaiming the Baptist Vision

# The Church

# Proclaiming the Baptist Vision

# The Church

Walter B. Shurden
editor

Smyth & Helwys Publishing, Inc.®
Macon, Georgia

ISBN 1-57312-024-3

*Proclaiming the Baptist Vision*
*The Church*

Walter B. Shurden, editor

Copyright © 1996
Smyth & Helwys Publishing, Inc.®

6316 Peake Road
Macon, Georgia 31210-3960
1-800-568-1248

*Library of Congress Cataloging-in-Publication Data*

The church / Walter B. Shurden, editor.
   (Proclaiming the Baptist vision; v. 3)
   vi + 154 pp.          6" x 9" (15 x 23 cm.)
   Includes bibliographical references.
   ISBN 1-57312-024-3 (alk. paper)
   1. Baptists—Doctrines.
   2. Baptists—Sermons.
   3. Sermons, American.
   I. Shurden, Walter B. II. Series.
   BX6331.2C58   1996
   262'.06—dc20               96-17330
                                CIP

# Contents

# Introduction

## by Walter B. Shurden

My earliest memory of church is walking one Sunday morning with my brother and cousins from our home on Third Street a few blocks away to the First Baptist Church in Greenwood, Mississippi. When I was a grammar school student, my family was not heavily invested in church at that time in our lives. But apparently I had been to church at least a few times, because I held a small, paperback Sunday school "quarterly" in my hands along with a Bible. I think I can yet take you near the spot where I distinctly remember thinking, "This feels good; going to church is a good thing to do." Growing up in Southern culture in the United States, few ever escape that sentiment completely. Nor should they. But for me it did not take! I soon became a dropout, what third-century Christians called a part of the "lapsed." My first memory about church, however, is that going to church felt good. Pride—the self-righteous kind—was my first churchly emotion.

I was "lapsed" great big until my first year of college. In the spring of 1955, after—to use Peter Marshall's tender phrase—"God tapped me on the shoulder," church became central in my life. By now we lived in Greenville, not Greenwood, Mississippi, still, however, in the fertile delta where cotton grew tall and reigned over everything else except high school football. And the sanctuary for my newfound faith became Second Baptist Church on South Theobald. What South Theobald meant in Greenville culture, "Second" Baptist meant in Baptist culture. "Second Baptist Church" often means "second" in terms of chronology. More often, however, it signals a decidedly non-elitist socioeconomic status overreaching the English language and called "middle class." "Po Folks" is closer to the truth.

With carpetless concrete floors at Second Baptist Church, we had cushionless pews, unrobed choirs (we knew liberalism when we saw it!), boisterous gospel singing, loud evangelistic preaching, and a place that felt unspeakably, indescribably good to me. The only appropriate word to describe the place is one we at Second Baptist would never have thought of using and truthfully probably did not know. The word is "sanctuary." It means a holy or sacred place, a refuge, an asylum, a shelter. More than anything else, this "sanctuary" consisted of a somewhat uneducated, more than somewhat unwealthy, lily-white, uncritical people who claimed to hate sin and Satan but love God, Jesus, the Bible, each other, and me.

What made Second Baptist Church feel unspeakably and indescribably good, of course, was overwhelmingly personal. Either those people loved me, believed in me, wanted the best for me, or they have deceived me to this very day. I have always, of course, believed the former. Looking back over my shoulder after more than forty years, I realize now how much at eighteen I resembled all eighteen-year-olds, thinking secretly that I was nobody and wanting so very much to be somebody.

Reverberating within the walls of that carpetless sanctuary of Second Baptist Church on South Theobald in Greenville, Mississippi, I heard the whispers of those delightful people, "You are!, You are!," "You are somebody!" They launched me with love! They launched me not only into life but also into the ministry of Jesus Christ. For the three years I was at Mississippi College in undergraduate school, that church sent a check every month to the college's finance office to help pay my tuition. Moreover, they did it for the other seven ministerial students who came out of that church during the same period of time.

My saga in Baptist churches is as diverse as Baptist life itself. I've worshiped "high," "low," and "broad" in Baptist churches; sung out of both the front and the back of the hymnal; preached in coatless short sleeve dress shirt in rural frame buildings as well as pulpit robe in urban cathedrals; baptized in cow ponds, cold rivers, and warm "indoor" baptismal pools; and been part of Sunday morning worship that closed with as much as forty-three stanzas of "Just As I Am" and as little as a brief benediction.

I came out of Second Baptist in Greenville, Mississippi, but I spent several years at both St. Charles in New Orleans, Lousiana, and Crescent Hill in Louisville, Kentucky, and even a couple of months at Myers Park in Charlotte, North Carolina. To say it historically for those who know the references, I came out of Sandy Creek, but I have been to Charleston. I apologize for neither and am grateful Baptists have been "catholic" enough to have both and all shades in between. Nor do the preachers, all of whom are Baptists, of the sermons included in this volume apologize. This book of sermons speaks *of* and *to* the Baptist understanding of church with its bewildering diversity.

The third of a five-volume series entitled *Proclaiming the Baptist Vision*, this volume focuses on the church. The first volume, published in 1993, highlights the Baptist emphasis on the priesthood of all believers, while the second volume, published in 1994, centers on the Bible. Two future volumes will concentrate on the Baptist principle of religious liberty and the Baptist view of the ordinances of baptism and the Lord's Supper.

Each volume in the series consists primarily of sermons. In addition to the sermons, however, each volume contains an introduction and a concluding essay. The essay provides the reader a historical\ theological context for understanding the specific issue under examination. My article entitled "The Priesthood of All Believers and Pastoral Authority in Baptist Thought" supplied the historical\theological foundation for clarifying that particular issue in volume one. In the second volume, *Proclaiming the Baptist Vision: The Bible*, I used Hugh Wamble's notable article "Baptists, the Bible, and Authority." In the present volume I employ "The Baptist Doctrine of the Church," a magnificent statement issued by the British Baptist Union in 1948. A brief introduction to the statement is included in chapter 16. Do not let the fact that this essay is fifty years-old keep you from a careful and critical study. It is one of the clearest statements on the Baptist perspective of church available.

My goal in the series is to present historic Baptist convictions in substantive sermonic form by some of Baptists' best preachers. The fifteen sermons in this particular volume will, I am confident, assist both laity and clergy in understanding better the Baptist interpretation of the church. Clergy often need literature stripped of theological*ese* regarding issues in Baptist life to place in the hands of laity. These five volumes are designed precisely to meet that need.

Moreover, I would be bold to say that I hope preachers themselves will find models and materials within these sermons that will help them with their pulpit ministry. If communicating Baptist distinctives has any value at all, it should be done on Sunday morning at 11:00 A.M. That hour is our one real opportunity to reach our Baptist people with the message of the Baptist heritage. Homiletical laziness, a pervasive disease of the Christian pulpit, does not need encouragement. This and other volumes in this series are not designed to intensify that problem but to act as a stimulant to the preacher's creative efforts. I hope, therefore, that preachers utilize these sermons to enrich their own pulpit ministry.

Only a few Christian denominations continue to obsess over their uniqueness and chosenness. Baptists have flirted with the idea of their specialness on and off for much of their 400-year history. In nineteenth-century America, especially in the South, a movement known as Landmarkism elevated to orthodoxy the notion that Baptist churches were the only true churches. Based on a false reading of Baptist and Christian history and a highly distorted reading of a few biblical texts, Landmarkism cut a wide swath through Baptist land. You will find not a taint of Landmarkism's high-flying brags in these sermons. These fourteen Baptist preachers take pains to identify Baptist churches with the larger church of Jesus Christ.

Nor will you find in these sermons a trace of contemporary theological fundamentalism with its alleged hammer lock on truth. To the contrary, what you will discover in these pages, as illustrated in the powerful sermon by William Powell Tuck, is a far more humble approach to the mystery of God's revelation. Describing some contemporary American church styles of which Baptists should beware, Tuck bemoans one such model as "The Only Understanding of Truth Church." Humility, respect for others' opinions, and tolerance, however, should never be read from these pages as absence of conviction. As you read these sermons, you will see what I mean. Convictions are clear. And one of those convictions contends that Baptists do not have God in a Baptist box.

Then what convictions will you find in these sermons? In her inspired and inspiring sermon, Meg Hess claims that the local Baptist church of her youth "became the place where I learned the practice of holding opposites in creative tension." As you read these sermons you will discern several "opposites" held in creative tension. The following are some of the creative tensions of the Baptist vision of the church affirmed in these pages.

(1) *The Baptist vision of the church proclaims the essence of the church as both divine and human.* The British Baptist Union spoke to the divine nature of the church when it declared,

> The origin of the Church is in the Gospel—in the mighty acts of God, the Incarnation, Ministry, Death, Resurrection, and Ascension of our Lord and the Descent of the Holy Spirit. Thus it is the power of God in Christ which created the Church and which sustains it through the centuries.

Internationally recognized Baptist church historian Leon McBeth preaches as superbly as he researches and writes the Baptist heritage. In his lead sermon in this volume, McBeth speaks of the church as a "spiritual community," by which he means the church has a divine rootage, a spiritual foundation. While very much a part of this world, the church is also something from "out of this world." Echoing the British statement, McBeth says,

> Human in membership, the church has a divine basis in Jesus Christ. The church is far more than a social club or human organization. People may join the church, but they do not create it. The church *is*; it exists by virtue of the life, death, and resurrection of Jesus Christ.

One of the brightest younger preaching talents among Baptists is Guy G. Sayles, Jr., the only individual with two sermons in this volume. Accentuating the divine essence of the church, Sayles says that the church is "all about Jesus." Sayles quotes Jürgen Moltmann to stress the divine dimension of the church. Among other things, Moltmann says that "the church's first and most significant word is not 'church' but Christ."

The Christian community affirms the divine character of the church as a part of its "faith" statements. One needs no faith, however, to claim that the church is also very human! Baptists acknowledge that the church is the community of the forgiven, not the community of the perfect.

Wallace Charles Smith, pastor of the Shiloh Baptist Church in Washington, D.C., and a Baptist preacher of renown, speaks indirectly to the human aspect of the church with his call for repentance in the church. While Smith's sermon could be classified as evangelistic, it is only so if one keeps in mind that Smith is "evangelizing" the church. Baptists adhere, says Smith, to the so-called Protestant Principle, the idea that the church must constantly be reformed. And so, Daniel Vestal, pastor of the Tallowood Baptist Church in Houston, Texas, and prominent Baptist leader, describes the church as being composed of "flawed" people. Throughout these sermons you will hear the echo, "The church is divine; the church is human."

(2) *The Baptist vision of the church proclaims the nature of the church as both universal and local.* In *The Baptist Doctrine of the Church* the British Baptist Union uttered an unambiguous identification of Baptists with what they called "the one holy catholic Church of our Lord Jesus Christ." Proclaiming the universality of the church, the Union said,

> Although Baptists have for so long held a position separate from that of other communions, they have always claimed to be part of the one holy catholic Church of our Lord Jesus Christ. They believe in the catholic Church as the holy society of believers in our Lord Jesus Christ, which He founded, of which He is the only Head, and in which He dwells by

His Spirit, so that though manifested in many communions, organized in various modes, and scattered throughout the world, it is yet one in Him.

The British statement continued, however, by claiming that the universal church manifests itself in local settings. "It is in membership of a local church in one place that the fellowship of the one holy catholic Church becomes significant," said the statement. And it added, "Indeed, such gathered companies of believers are the local manifestation of the one Church of God on earth and in heaven."

The emphasis that the church is both universal and local will be found in most of the sermons in this volume. McBeth, Sayles, Brown, O' Brien, Tyler, and Vestal, among others, reflect this theme. More than a theoretical affirmation, this dualistic emphasis contains several significant implications for Baptist church life spelled out in these sermons.

(3) *The Baptist vision of the church proclaims the membership of the church to consist of people who are both believers and disciples.* This dual emphasis is crucial if we are to recover the Baptist vision of the church. "Believing" in Christ and "following" Christ are, if we read the New Testament correctly, inseparable.

Baptists often initiate their discussion of the church by asserting that they emerged in seventeenth-century England trying to restore a "believers' church." What do Baptists mean by such language? They mean that the church should be composed only of those people who could make a conscious and voluntary confession of faith in Christ. Baptism, therefore, was restricted to "believers." Elaborating upon this concept with expressive language, *The Baptist Doctrine of the Church* put it this way:

The basis of our membership in the church is a conscious and deliberate acceptance of Christ as Saviour and Lord by each individual. There is, we hold, a personal crisis in the soul's life when a person stands alone in God's presence, responds to God's gracious activity, accepts His forgiveness, and commits to the Christian way of life. Such a crisis may be swift and emotional or slow-developing and undramatic, and is normally experienced within and because of our life in the Christian community, but it is always a personal experience wherein God offers His salvation in Christ, and the individual, responding by faith, receives the assurance of the Spirit that by grace he or she is the child of God. It is this vital evangelical experience which underlies the Baptist conception of the Church and is both expressed and safeguarded by the sacrament of Believer's Baptism.

Alan Neely, a former Baptist missionary and now Baptist professor of ecumenics and missions at Princeton Theological Seminary, reflects on the issue of "believer's baptism" and raises provocative questions in his sermon concerning the Baptist distinctive. Does the historic Baptist emphasis on "believer's baptism" help Baptists today, asks Neely, to produce more believers or more committed believers than Christian groups who do not subscribe to "believer's baptism"? Neely is concerned with a crucial issue in Baptist church life—the vitality of local Baptist churches. How do we revitalize the meaning of church membership in contemporary Baptist life when we speak so cavalierly about numerous non-resident and inactive members? Can meaningful church membership be renewed? How?

Neely's questions suggest that Baptists may have unwittingly separated serious discipleship and disciplined church membership from our initial emphasis on believer's baptism. Might we be duped into thinking that simply because we repeat the words, "believer's baptism," "a regenerate church," and other such Baptist slogans, that we have actually duplicated the intent behind those words?

Neely's concern did not escape the attention of those who drafted *The Baptist Doctrine of the Church* fifty years ago. With their emphasis on a believers' church, they also stressed the importance of ongoing discipleship. Quoting from the 1677 London Confession, they said:

> Membership was not regarded as a private option, for the CONFESSION continues: "All believers are bound to join themselves to particular churches when and where they have opportunity so to do." In our tradition discipleship involves both church membership and a full acceptance of the idea of churchmanship.

You will find this dual concern for a believers' church and a disciples' church expressed in diverse ways in most of the sermons in this book. One fact is clear from these sermons. Baptists never interpreted "believer's baptism" as a frivolous nod to a creedal statement. If "faith" is not "following," and if believers are not disciples, all of the Baptist talk of a regenerate church membership is little more than ancient theological words blowing in the contemporary wind.

(4) *The Baptist vision of the church proclaims the government of the church as both a Christocracy and a democracy.* Generally speaking, three basic types of church government exist among Christian denominations. They are episcopal, presbyterian, and congregational. In episcopal church government authority is placed in the hands of one person,

usually a bishop. In presbyterian church government, authority is vested in a small group, often called elders, within the local church. In congregational church government, authority is placed in the hands of all the members of the local church. To say it another way, in episcopal church government you have a spiritual monarchy, in presbyterian church government a spiritual oligarchy, and in congregational church government a spiritual democracy.

Baptists always have been and should always remain congregational and democratic in church order. Honesty compels us to acknowledge, however, that the New Testament does not describe in detail precisely how the churches should be structured. Proof texts from various parts of the New Testament may be called on to support all three types mentioned above.

When Baptists began in seventeenth-century England, they were seeking to get out from under the authority of bishops and other ecclesiastical officials and restore the authority of church life to the entire membership of each local congregation. A spiritual democracy best expressed Baptist concerns respecting the equality of the laity with the clergy, the value of each individual in the church's life, and the importance of the group discovery of the will of God.

Much is said in the sermons in this volume both explicitly and implicitly about how Baptist churches govern themselves. All of the preachers of these sermons agree that Baptists should be congregational and democratic in government. They also underscore a second emphasis, however. While a local church is completely free from both civil and ecclesiastical external authorities, a local church, as McBeth says, "lives and works under the absolute lordship of Jesus Christ." In other words, a Baptist church functions as a democracy, but it strives to be a Christocracy.

Again, *The Baptist Doctrine of the Church* says it well:

> The church meeting, though outwardly a democratic way of ordering the affairs of the church, has deeper significance. It is the occasion when, as individuals and as a community, we submit ourselves to the guidance of the Holy Spirit and stand under the judgments of God that we may know what is the mind of Christ. We believe that the structure of local churches just described springs from the gospel and best preserves its essential features.

Baptist democracy is really a strategy of getting at the mind of Christ. Baptists do not claim that the goal of their polity is unique among other Christian groups. Surely all Christian churches seek the mind of

Christ and the will of God, but Baptists believe that democracy is the most theologically appropriate way of arriving at the divine will.

(5) *The Baptist vision of the church proclaims local churches as both sanctuaries of individual freedom and sacred places of communal responsibility.* A fundamental point of tension in Baptist church life concerns the freedom of the individual and the identity and authority of the community. Without question, a strong sense of individualism exists in Baptist life. To deny or ignore that fact skews the Baptist witness. Also without question, a local Baptist church constitutes a single entity with some specific identity.

You will discover the preachers of these sermons inevitably struggling with the bipolar tension of individualism and community in Baptist church life. Howard Roberts, the creative pastor of the First Baptist Church in Auburn, Alabama, accents individualism while recognizing the role of community. He interprets the Baptist doctrine of the church within the context of the priesthood of believers.

In his sermon, "The Church: The Faces of Christ," Guy Sayles underscores the role of community without sacrificing the rights of the individual. "Nearly every New Testament snapshot of the church is a group photo," says Sayles. And he adds, "There are very few individual portraits." Supporting his point of view with his reading of Baptist history, Sayles asserts:

> As passionate as our forebears were in their promotion and protection of individual liberty of conscience, they also were keenly aware of the need for such individual liberty to find nurture, expression, and accountability in the community of faith. They insisted on freedom, and they exercised that freedom by willingly binding themselves to the covenant community.

Bill O'Brien is currently one of Baptists' best students of the mission of the church. In an intriguing sermon interpreting the confluence of the Baptist distinctives of freedom and missions, O'Brien warns of excessive individualism. At times in Baptist life, he argues, privacy, piety, and freedom end up being used to justify isolation and insulation, or it emboldens a person or group to act without reference to the rest of the body of Christ. Our freedoms, he asserts, are limited by our self-imposed covenants of commitment. O'Brien's sermon title, "Free To Serve," indicates his point of view.

John Tyler, a layman, takes something of the same approach. In a sermon that brilliantly models how to preach a single sermon on an entire book in the Bible, he peers beyond the issues in the Corinthian church to a fundamental issue confronting Paul. Tyler believes that Paul's basic dilemma in 1 Corinthians is not speaking in tongues or eating meat offered to idols or other isolated issues, but the more foundational concern of personal freedom versus communal responsibility. Tyler concludes where Paul concludes: freedom is a servant of the community.

Maybe the most artistic and moving sermon in this entire volume comes from the life and pen of Meg Hess. A beautiful testimonial of growing up Baptist, Hess's sermon centers on the issue of the ordination of women for ministry and the inevitable tension between an individual's call from God and the church's recognition of that call. "Church, from my early childhood," she says, "was a study in the creation and maintenance of an atmosphere where the tenuous balance of Soul Freedom could be lived out in community." Individualism and community as opposites held in creative tension appear repeatedly in these sermons.

(6) *The Baptist vision of the church proclaims the ministry of the church in terms of the priesthood of all believers, including the roles of both laity and clergy.* Daniel Carro, one of the influential voices of Baptists in Latin America, implores Baptists in his sermon to create an "open" church for facing the future. Part of that openness for Carro involves the concept and practice of the priesthood of all believers. Carro wants Baptists to be open to what he calls the "interior" world of the churches. He explains:

> A church open to its interior world is a church open to all of its members, regardless of class, gender, color, or previous religious background. It is a church open to all voices, interests, and points of view. Next to closing itself off to God's spirit, the church does itself the greatest harm by closing itself off to the whole of its membership. When a church centers on a ruling pastor, a dominant group, or a controlling bureaucracy —that is the beginning of the end of God's church in that place.

Howard Roberts also strikes a strong note for the priesthood of all believers in his sermon "How Baptists Do Church." Indeed, Roberts believes you do not understand the Baptist way of doing church if you ignore or minimize the historic Baptist notion of believers' priesthood. Roberts, more than any other person contributing to this volume, enumerates the implications of the priesthood of all believers for the Baptist vision of the church.

The document of the Baptist Union of Great Britain and Ireland also speaks to the issue of the priesthood of all believers. "The worship, preaching, sacramental observances, fellowship and witness are all congregational acts of the whole church in which each member shares responsibility," says the historic document, "for all are held to be of equal standing in Christ, though there is a diversity of gifts and a difference of functions."

The British essay then spells out what "equal standing in Christ" within the church means for the Baptist concept of the ministry:

> The Baptist conception of the ministry is governed by the principle that it is a ministry of a church and not only a ministry of an individual. It is the church which preaches the Word and celebrates the sacraments, and it is the church which, through pastoral oversight, feeds the flock and ministers to the world. It normally does these things through the person of its minister, but not solely through the minister. Any member of the church may be authorized by it, on occasion, to exercise the functions of the ministry, in accordance with the principle of the priesthood of all believers, to preach the Word, to administer baptism, to preside at the Lord's table, to visit, and comfort or rebuke members of the fellowship.

Baptist churches encourage the priesthood of all believers without deprecating the role of the professional ministry.

More than simply stress the equality between all believers in local churches, one sermon in this collection exemplifies that concept. If you have questions about the ability and gifts of laity to interpret and communicate Scripture in a genuinely creative and imaginative way, read John Tyler's sermon entitled "Back to Basics."

Much is often made in evangelical circles about "preaching through the Bible," by which is usually meant a verse-by-verse exegesis of the entire Bible. I am more and more impressed by sermons that seek to interpret an entire book in the Bible rather than a sermon that uses a single text that often distracts from the essential message of the book where the text is found. Often when the latter occurs, one misinterprets both the book and the text under consideration. British New Testament scholar N. T. Wright's sermons in *Following Jesus* (Eerdmans, 1994) provide some of the best examples of single sermons interpreting entire biblical books. John Tyler does the same with his ingenious recreation of the Corinthian situation. Tyler not only affirms the priesthood of all believers, he incarnates it.

One cannot speak of the importance of the priesthood of believers in contemporary Baptist life without reference to gender issues, especially the role of women in our churches. As indicated above, the sermon from Meg Hess both raises and addresses this issue in a representative way. Baptists will hopefully work and pray for the day when every young woman in every Baptist church can dream of an "L. D. Johnson" seated on the front row, leaning forward with eager anticipation on his face, saying, "Go ahead Meg, you have something to say." Baptists will not live out their convictions, distinctives, and heritage until that dream becomes a reality.

(7) *The Baptist vision of the church proclaims the mission of the church as both worship and witness.* The church exists for both inreach and outreach. As Daniel Carro says in his sermon, Baptist churches must be open to both their interior and exterior worlds. Part of the mission of the church has to do with life *within* the church, part with life *without*.

Maybe the most comprehensive statement in this volume of the Baptist vision of the mission of Baptist churches comes from the concluding historical\theological essay. It describes the task of the churches as follows:

> The life of a gathered Baptist church centres in worship, in the preaching of the Word, in the observance of the two sacraments of Believer's Baptism and the Lord's Supper, in growth in fellowship and in witness and service to the world outside.

A close examination of the previous sentence causes one, as does Leon McBeth, to summarize the mission of the church as "worship and witness."

Baptists doubtless have made too little out of that phrase often printed at the top of Christian worship bulletins: "The Divine Service of Worship." The worship of Almighty God *is* a form of the church's service to God. Baptist forms of worship differ widely, but the essay on *The Baptist Doctrine of the Church* was generally on target when it said:

> Our forms of worship are in the Reformed tradition and are not generally regulated by liturgical forms. Our tradition is one of spontaneity and freedom, but we hold that there should be disciplined preparation of every part of the service. The sermon, as an exposition of the Word of God and a means of building up the faith and life of the congregation, has a central place in public worship.

The statement contains several important emphases. "Not generally regulated by liturgical forms" has to do not only with established patterns of worship but also with the centrality of the altar or the sacramental meal. As a matter of fact, many Baptist churches have discovered a new spiritual vitality within the last twenty-five years through a more liturgical form of worship, especially in following the Christian calendar for seasons of worship. While spontaneity and freedom characterize the Baptist tradition and lead to endless diversity in Baptist life, Baptists have historically stressed that "there should be disciplined preparation of every part of the service." Biblical exposition is central to Baptist worship.

William Powell Tuck, a longtime pastor and teacher of preaching and worship, has a passionate concern that Baptist worship properly praise the Eternal God. In his sermon he decries what he calls "The Warm Feeling, Friendly, Everybody-Always-Happy, Noncontroversial, Easygoing, Crowd-Pleasing, Entertaining Church." In this church, says Tuck,

> Worship services are planned primarily for their entertainment value. The more the spectators feel they have been entertained, the more they think they have worshiped. When they leave this church, they want to feel warm and cozy inside. The worship of Almighty God becomes the theological equivalent of a Lawrence Welk *Variety Hour* with the humor and theological depth of *Hee Haw* and the excitement of a NCAA basketball championship. This church focuses primarily on entertaining us and making us feel satisfied.

To confuse sublime worship with superficial entertainment harms the mission of the church as a worshiping community.

The church lives to worship. It also lives to witness. And the witness includes both verbal and nonverbal forms. Leon McBeth underscores the fact that the body of Christ is left with a "Great Commission." This commission, he says, "gives marching orders to the church to witness for Christ throughout the world, seeking to win people to faith in Christ." Guy Sayles, among others in this volume, joins McBeth's evangelistic emphasis. "We need the church," says Sayles, "because the church keeps telling the story." And then he makes the application to all of us:

> Most of us would not have experienced the grace of Jesus Christ had there not been people who cared enough to tell us the story. Those people who showed us and shared with us the gospel were church people,

people who were sustained and challenged by the community to demonstrate and declare the love of God revealed in Jesus Christ. The vast majority of us would not be Christian had it not been for the people who make up the church.

If the witness of the church involves word and speaking, it also includes service and ministering. Lavonn Brown, pastor of the First Baptist Church in Norman, Oklahoma, for almost thirty years, and Brad Creed, the gifted young dean at Truett Theological Seminary in Waco, Texas, serve in a geographical area of the Baptist world where verbal witnessing is stressed as a major function of the church. Both Brown and Creed remind us in their sermons, however, of the equally important nonverbal witness of the church. Lavonn Brown and Brad Creed hold up for Baptists today the ministry of the life of Jesus as a model of the church's task.

Creed speaks of the church in his sermon as "The Servant People of God." He describes their ministry:

> The servant people of God roll up their sleeves and use their training in humility to get involved with people in their difficulties. They bind wounds, wipe away tears, and embrace the unlovable. If the church desires greatness, it pursues greatness by the route of servanthood. Sometimes Jesus leads his church to people who are lost, hurting, confused, and otherwise difficult to deal with. Servanthood compels the church to identify with people as Jesus did.

And Brown, a model Baptist pastor, urges the church in contemporary society to become a fellowship of loving concern where "tears are understood and heart cries are heard," where "spirits can take wings," where "questions can be asked," and where "failures are not final."

The sermons in this book do not constitute *the* Baptist vision of the church. Given Baptist diversity within America and around the world, no such singular approach to Baptist life exists. You will even find minor differences or emphases among the contributors to this particular volume. Despite such disagreements, however, you will discover within these pages the conviction that Baptists have a vision of the church worth saving for today and tomorrow. Because it is a vision worth saving, it is certainly a vision worth preaching.

# The Church
# Community of Faith

## H. Leon McBeth

He said to them, "But who do you say that I am?" Simon Peter answered, "You are the Messiah, the Son of the living God." And Jesus answered him, "Blessed are you, Simon son of Jonah! For flesh and blood has not revealed this to you, but my Father in heaven. And I tell you, you are Peter, and on this rock I will build my church, and the gates of Hades will not prevail against it. I will give you the keys of the kingdom of heaven, and whatever you bind on earth will be bound in heaven, and whatever you loose on earth will be loosed in heaven." Then he sternly ordered the disciples not to tell anyone that he was the Messiah. (Matt 16:15-20)

God put this power to work in Christ when he raised him from the dead and seated him at his right hand in the heavenly places, far above all rule and authority and power and dominion, and above every name that is named, not only in this age but also in the age to come. And he has put all things under his feet and has made him the head over all things for the church, which is his body, the fullness of him who fills all in all. (Eph 1:20-23)

> I love thy kingdom, Lord,
> The house of thine abode,
> The church our blest Redeemer saved,
> With his own precious blood.[1]

For generations Baptists have sung this hymn as an expression of their commitment to Christ and his church. Aside from its too easy identification of church and kingdom of God, these words form a good summary of the Baptist vision of the church.

The church is a community. The Greek word for church, *ekklesia*, means a gathering or coming together. Early Christians often spoke of themselves as *koinonia*, a fellowship. In modern times, Baptists often refer to the "church family," spotlighting that the church is a koinonia fellowship. As Christians we are members of the family of God, and we express that family relationship in the Father's house, the church.

## The Church: A Spiritual Community

In Ephesians 1:22-23, the writer proclaims that God has made Christ "the head over all things for the church, which is his body." Human in membership, the church has a divine basis in Jesus Christ. The church is far more than a social club or human organization. People may join the church, but they do not create it. The church *is*; it exists by virtue of the life, death, and resurrection of Jesus Christ. To some extent, which the theologians have never quite worked out, the church is a continuing incarnation of Jesus Christ in the world. As Paul expressed it, "the church, which is his body."

Politicians seeking votes often regard the church as merely another voluntary organization. People seeking standing and prestige may regard the church as a socially respected institution where they can meet the right kind of people. But the church is profoundly more than just another social club that happens to meet on Sundays. Despite its human membership, the church has a divine basis in Jesus Christ. It is a spiritual community.

## The Church: A Believing Community

One of the earliest Baptist confessions of faith says,

> The church of CHRIST is a company of faithful people . . . separated from the world by the word & Spirit of God, . . . being knit unto the Lord, & one unto another, by Baptism . . . Upon their own confession of the faith.[2]

According to early Baptists, it is believer's baptism that knits us into the fabric of the family of God. Believers become a part of the church "upon their own confession of faith."

Baptists have from the first insisted upon a *believers' church*. Each person must make a personal decision to repent of sins and receive Jesus Christ as Savior and Lord. In Baptist theology, there is no room for proxy faith. For centuries, Baptist sermons have called for personal faith and a personal decision for Christ, a decision that no one else can make for the individual.

Toward the close of his earthly ministry, Christ asked his disciples a crucial question, "Who do people say that the Son of Man is?" (Matt 16:13). Jesus sought feedback to see how much of his message had gotten through. Simon Peter, informal spokesman for the group, replied with a summary of popular public perception about Jesus. Some people, Peter reported, thought Christ was a new embodiment of Elijah or Jeremiah, or perhaps some other prophet. All of these were positive reports; Peter refrained from saying that some thought Christ was demon-possessed (John 8:42). But even these answers, though complimentary, were not adequate, and Christ pressed the issue. "But who do you say that I am?" (Matt 16:15).

This led to one of the most crucial pronouncements of Christ, one that has given rise to much misunderstanding. Peter replied, "You are the Messiah, the Son of the living God." Here is a brief summary of the Christian faith: Jesus is the Christ. To that confession Christ responded, apparently with joy,

> Blessed are you, Simon son of Jonah! For flesh and blood has not revealed this to you, but my Father in heaven. And I tell you, you are Peter, on this rock I will build my church and the gates of Hades will not prevail against it. (Matt 16:17-18)

"Upon this rock" the church is built. Early church theologians taught that the solid rock, the foundation of the church, is the lordship of Christ and Peter's confession of that lordship. However, by the fifth century some theologians said the rock refers to Peter, and thus the church is built upon Peter and his apostolic authority. The apostle Paul had no doubt that Jesus Christ is the foundation of faith; he said, "No one can lay any foundation other than the one that has been laid; that foundation is Jesus Christ" (1 Cor 3:11). Upon Peter's kind of committed faith in Christ the church was built, and that faith sustains the church to this day.

Many historians believe the search for a true church best explains Baptist origins as a separate denomination in the early seventeenth century. Baptists called for reforms in baptism, ministry, and worship; but their most basic search was for a biblical basis for a true church. They found that basis for a true church in the personal faith of believers.

Baptism of believers by immersion is important to Baptists. In their London Confession of 1644, Baptists said,

> Christ hath here on earth a spiritual Kingdom which is the Church . . . which Church, as it is visible to us, is a company of visible Saints, called and separated from the world by the word and Spirit of God, to the visible profession of the faith of the Gospel, being baptized into that faith and joined to the Lord and each other.[3]

Later in the same confession, they specified, "The way and manner of dispensing this Ordinance the Scripture holds out to be dipping or plunging the whole body under water."[4]

Many people assume that immersion is the central doctrine for Baptists, but that misses the point. For Baptists, the crucial point is that baptism be applied to *believers* as a mark of their personal faith in Christ. It is faith in Christ that knits us to Christ and to fellow believers in the church. If Baptists had to choose—which fortunately they do not—between baptism of believers and baptism by immersion, they must choose baptism of believers. It would be far better to sprinkle a believer than to immerse a nonbeliever.

## The Church: A Worshiping Community

I saw a church bulletin recently that said, "The church does not exist for those who are already members. The primary purpose of the church is to win those who are not yet members." Surely no one can doubt that the church has a biblical mandate to bear witness to unbelievers and win as many of them to faith in Christ as possible. According to biblical theology, however, is this the "first and foremost" reason the church exists?

W. T. Conner, conservative theologian of the Southwest, astonished some when he said that the primary purpose of the church is to worship God. The church must do many things, but the first thing it must do is provide an opportunity for believers to seek the presence of God in worship. There is room in the church for evangelism in winning new converts, for instruction in helping converts to grow in grace, and for promotion to enlist participation in the life of the church. However, if these activities, worthy as they are, crowd out quiet, concentrated communion with God, the church forfeits its first and foremost purpose.

At a Sunday night service in a West Texas church, a young pastor led the faithful in praise, prayers, Bible reading, and preaching. The Spirit of God seemed to draw near as the people reaffirmed their faith and renewed their allegiance to Christ. The service closed with an invitation, but no one came forward. After the service a layman, no doubt intending to encourage the pastor, said, "Well, preacher, nothing happened tonight, but you keep on trying. Maybe something will happen next time." When the pastor asked, "What do you mean, nothing happened," the layman seemed surprised, as if the answer was too obvious for comment. He replied, "Why, nobody came forward in the invitation."

In that layman's mind, unless somebody came forward to be converted or recommitted, the service was a failure in which "nothing happened." We have conditioned people to equate "public decisions" with successful church services. We often forget that important as public affirmations of faith are, the first and foremost purpose of the church is to worship God. When a church provides an opportunity for its members to catch a new glimpse of God in worship, that leads its members to deepen their prayer and devotional life, that leads them into a closer walk with the Savior, in that church truly something worthwhile has happened. First and foremost, the church is a worshiping community.

## The Church: A Witnessing Community

In the church worship is basic, but it is no substitute for witness. Both worship and witness have a rightful role. Christ's first word to his disciples after his resurrection was, "Go therefore and make disciples of all nations" (Matt 28:19). This "Great Commission," as we have called it, gives marching orders to the church to witness for Christ throughout the world, seeking to win people to faith in Christ. The Bible does not prescribe exactly how or by what methods the church should bear its witness. Methods may change over the years as conditions change. What does not change, however, is the biblical mandate for missions, to bear witness to Christ both near and far.

It was this biblical mandate for missions that took Baptist shoe cobbler William Carey to India, schoolteacher Lottie Moon to China, and physician Bill Wallace to China. Baptists are a *missionary* people who have given time and money, as well as their sons and daughters, to the missionary task of converting the nations. This missionary mandate was given primarily to the church, not just to individuals. It is part of the purpose and function of the church, as a church, to engage in witness to share the gospel from the local community to the far corners of the world.

It has been commonplace to say that the glue that holds Baptists together is missions. Evangelism at home and missions abroad, which are really the same task in different locations, have enlisted, motivated, inspired, and guided Baptist churches for generations. A story is told of an artist commissioned to paint a dead church. Many expected the artist to present a portrait of a church with dilapidated building, broken windows, and weed-grown yard. Instead, the resulting portrait of a dead church showed a beautiful building with every mark of success, but with a cobweb drawn over the box for missionary contributions. A church that neglects its witness to the world can hardly be counted successful, no matter what its other accomplishments.

## The Church: A Ministering Community

The world is full of hurting people, and many of them have no place to turn for help. The problems seem overwhelming, but the church must do what it can to help people in need. On his missionary journeys Paul brought back a relief offering for the poor of Jerusalem. The distribution of church assistance to the needy called forth the appointment of helpers that some have seen as the origin of deacons (Acts 6:1-6). On many occasions Jesus fed the hungry, healed the sick, and ministered to physical as well as spiritual needs of people.

One of the most pointed parables Jesus told concerned the Good Samaritan (Luke 10:30-37). The story concerned a traveler who fell victim to roadside bandits, a problem common then and not unknown today. A priest and a Levite, religious leaders who were possibly on their way to Jerusalem to fulfill their assigned rotation as worship leaders at the Temple, saw the Samaritan but passed by quickly to avoid involvement. But a lowly Samaritan saw the victim, had compassion upon him, and at some personal risk and cost to himself came to the rescue of the man in need. Perhaps the priest and Levite felt sorry for the victim, but they were too busy with their own activities to stop and render aid.

Obviously the church today cannot feed all the world's hungry, cloth all the ragged, or heal all the sick. But the church that does nothing, that completely ignores the hungry and homeless and helpless all about, is missing a vital ingredient of what church is supposed to be. On one occasion Jesus said,

> I was hungry and you gave me food, I was thirsty and you gave me something to drink, I was a stranger and you welcomed me, I was naked and you gave me clothing, I was sick and you took care of me, I was in prison and you visited me. (Matt 25:35-36)

But the faithful searched their memory and said, in effect, "Lord, when was that? We can't seem to recall." Christ startled them all by saying, "Truly, I tell you, just as you did it to one of the least of these who are members of my family, you did it to me" (Matt 25:40).

If Jesus Christ should appear on our doorstep today hungry, cold, and sick, surely any Christian among us would gladly offer food, or clothing, or shelter. But the glorified Christ today has no need of a sandwich or blanket from us. But many people do need these things, and Jesus said that when we help people in need, it is as if we help Christ himself.

To fulfil its biblical mandate, a church must do what it can to help people in need. A church that spends all its resources on fine buildings, numerous personnel, and extensive programs to the total neglect of people in need is not fulfilling its mission as a ministering community. There are drawbacks, however. The church whose ultimate god is numerical growth should be cautious about ministering to people in need. People in need seldom augment budgets and do not always inflate statistics of church growth.

## The Church: An Autonomous Community

Here is a paradox: the church lives and works under the absolute lordship of Jesus Christ, and yet the church is completely free to determine its own affairs. Some describe Baptist church polity as "spiritual democracy," but this may not be the best description. By spiritual democracy, we do not mean the church is free to do anything the members want; instead, it means that the church is free to obey the will of Christ as best it can determine what that will is. It means that all of the members, and not just the minister or deacons or some committee, have a role in seeking the will of Christ.

Churches in New Testament times exercised freedom and autonomy. They chose their own leaders (Acts 1:15-26), decided cases of church discipline (Matt 18:15-18), and launched programs of witness and mission (Acts 13:1-3). In none of these cases did they seek the permission or approval of others.

It is clear that in New Testament churches, all the members shared in decision making. Baptists have sought to follow that biblical pattern in their church life. Unlike churches that vest all authority in a bishop or minister, Baptists have preferred a form of church democracy in which all the members, under the lordship of Christ, have a voice.

The idea that the pastor is the "ruler of the church" has appeared in Baptist life only recently, and is a gross perversion of the early biblical and Baptist theology of ministry.

As an autonomous community, the church must remain separate from the state. In Matthew 22:21 Jesus said we should "give therefore to the emperor the things that are the emperor's, and to God the things that are God's." There Jesus, who had been asked about paying taxes to Rome, indicated that Christians have duties both to God and to civil government, but these are different duties. The great Baptist pastor George W. Truett quoted that verse and said, "That utterance, once for all, marked the divorcement of church and state."[5]

In America, Baptists had a leading role in winning religious liberty for all and guarding that liberty by separation of church and state. That freedom and church/state separation are embedded in the First Amendment. Baptists believe that church/state separation is biblical, and that it is better for the well-being of both church and state.

## The Church: A World Community

When Baptists say "church," they usually mean a local body with a specific name and address. Mostly the New Testament uses "church" in the local sense, as the church in Phillipi or the church in Corinth. The Bible, however, also uses the word "church" in a larger sense, to designate the people of God everywhere. Sometimes in our writings we designate the local body as "church," lower case, while the world-wide community of believers is written "Church."

What is the relationship of a church to the Church? While the local body of believers has complete freedom and autonomy to determine its own affairs, call its own ministers, own its own property, and determine its own ministry projects, yet they must also recognize that they are part of a much larger movement. One of the earliest Baptist associations in a pioneer statement on church polity and cooperation said, "That particular churches of Christ ought to hold a firm communion each with other," because "all the particular assembleys [churches] are but one Mount Zion."[6] This pioneer statement of Baptist polity and autonomy emphasizes not only the *independence*, but the *interdependence* of churches. There is no good reason for a Baptist church to take a "Lone Ranger" approach and refuse to relate to other churches.

For the same reasons, many Baptists have long realized that Baptists are not the only true Christians in the world, and that Baptists can and should find suitable ways to cooperate with believers in other denominations for common causes. While they have been cautious about the entanglements of the modern ecumenical movement, there is every reason for Baptist churches to acknowledge and act upon their sense of common identity with other believers who bear other denominational labels. If not always structurally, certainly spiritually, the many churches are all part of the one Church.

"I love thy kingdom, Lord." If we really mean it, we cannot neglect the church. Even with its human blemishes and historic blunders, in the church there is much to love.

## Notes

[1]Timothy Dwight, "I Love Thy Kingdom, Lord."

[2]Thomas Helwys, "A Declaration of Faith," 1611, reprinted in William L. Lumpkin, *Baptist Confessions of Faith* (Valley Forge PA: Judson Press, 1959) 116f. Spelling and punctuation modernized.

[3]Lumpkin, 165. Spelling modernized.

[4]Ibid., 167.

[5]George W. Truett, "Baptists and Religious Liberty," sermon delivered in Washington DC, 16 May 1920, reprinted in H. Leon McBeth, ed., *A Sourcebook for Baptist Heritage* (Nashville: Broadman Press, 1990) 471.

[6]Minutes of Abingdon Association, October 1652, reprinted in McBeth, 62-63.

# The Church Committed to Christ

## Guy G. Sayles, Jr.

And so, brothers and sisters, I could not speak to you as spiritual people, but rather as people of the flesh, as infants in Christ. I fed you with milk, not solid food, for you were not ready for solid food. Even now you are still not ready, for you are still of the flesh. For as long as there is jealousy and quarreling among you, are you not of the flesh, and behaving according to human inclinations? For when one says, "I belong to Paul," and another, "I belong to Apollos," are you not merely human?

What then is Apollos? What is Paul? Servants through whom you came to believe, as the Lord assigned to each. I planted, Apollos waters, but God gave the growth. So neither the one who plants nor the one who waters is anything, but only God who gives the growth. The one who plants and the one who waters have a common purpose, and each will receive wages according to the labor of each. For we are God's servants, working together; you are God's field, God's building.

According to the grace of God given to me, like a skilled master builder I laid a foundation, and someone else is building on it. Each builder must choose with care how to build on it. For no one can lay any foundation other than the one that has been laid; that foundation is Jesus Christ. Now if anyone builds on the foundation with gold, silver, precious stones, wood, hay, straw—the work of each builder will become visible, for the Day will disclose it, because it will be revealed with fire, and the fire will test what sort of work each has done. If what has been built on the foundation survives, the builder will receive a reward. If the work is burned up, the builder will suffer loss; the builder will be saved, but only as through fire. (1 Cor 3:1-15)

Over the span of my now thoroughly middle-aged life, I have cycled through quite a number of views and opinions about the church. My childhood memories of the First Baptist Church in Conley, Georgia—where I was baptized, where I wore the patches and badges of a Royal Ambassador, and where I first heard the whispers of a calling to ministry—are almost uniformly positive. The people of that church were my extended family; I learned to call many of the men and women of that church "uncle" or "aunt." Their homes and hearts were open to me.

I was too young and too naive to sense any of the inevitable tensions that are part of any group's life together; and, besides, while business meetings were in session, we were in children's choirs. Worship was hardly ever dull, in part because I was so captivated by the idea that Jesus Christ, who had been crucified so long ago, was, in fact, alive and walking around the church while we were singing and listening to the sermon. If Jesus might, at any moment, tap me on the shoulder and say something to me, how could worship ever be dull? The excitement of it all did not make me a model citizen. I did my share of note-passing and gum-chewing, but even when I was "cutting up" (as my parents called it), I knew that Jesus had his eyes on me. From first grade, when we started attending church, until age fourteen, when my parents abruptly stopped participating, I was convinced that the church was virtually perfect.

When I got my driver's license and could go to church by myself, I made sporadic attempts to find a place in various churches; but I did not connect with one. Because of the kinds of emotional struggles and intellectual difficulties that many adolescents have, I experienced a gradual loss of faith. It's a common story, so it is enough to say that I asked questions that no one in the churches I attended as a teenager seemed willing to answer. In those days, I concluded that the church was an irrelevant relic that depended on the collective illusions of people who were willingly shut off from the great big world beyond the church's red-brick walls and colonial columns.

In college, through a series of events I can only call providential, I got my faith back, or the faith got me back. With renewed faith, I also heard once again God's call to ministry, and, of course, back to church. Off to seminary Anita and I went, full of idealism and hope; and, of course—and I'll speak only for myself—an unconscious but deep need for affirmation and an unacknowledged but driving ambition.

## The Church and the Religion of Big Ideas

Since seminary days, I have held to numerous and sometimes contradictory models of the church and ministry. Looking back, I know that I thought of the church as irrelevant and of ministry as my calling to make it relevant. To make it relevant, I first tried the Religion of Big Ideas. The trouble with the church, I reasoned, was that it wasn't intellectual enough. It was weighed down with a lot of pietistic folk religion and naive emotionalism—vestiges of revivalism that churches in the South never quite got over. All the church needed was to be delivered from the darkness of ignorance. There was nothing wrong with the church that a good strong dose of philosophical theology couldn't cure. The church could, with its thinking straightened out, become a force to reckon with in the modern world.

## The Church and the Religion of Big Causes

When the church wasn't transformed by information, I turned from the Religion of Big Ideas to the Religion of Big Causes. The trouble with the church, I decided, was that it wasn't relevant to modern social problems. It wasn't sufficiently activist. It was hindered by its cultural captivity to bourgeois values, by its cold loyalty to cash and capitalism, and by its knee-jerk nationalism. Now, however, with my knowledge of Marx (Karl *and* Groucho), and with Saul Alinsky's guidebook in hand, I would open the blind eyes of the church people, show them the world as it really is, and get them involved in making a difference. There was nothing wrong with the church that a demonstration, a petition, and a boycott wouldn't cure.

## The Church and the Religion of the Big Deal

When the church wasn't transformed by activism, I flirted, briefly, with the Religion of the Big Deal. The reason that the church seemed irrelevant to the culture was that it wasn't offering the kinds of things people were interested in. It wasn't strong enough and big enough to make an impression. In a *Doonesbury* cartoon, Mike is talking with the pastor of "The Little Church of Walden":

> "So, how'd your new church get started, Rev?"
Pastor: "Aerobics."
Mike: "Aerobics?"
Pastor: "I needed something to attract folks from the community. The focus group suggested an aerobics class. It worked, so I added yoga and bingo, and then a few 12-Step programs, and then we opened a soup kitchen, which led to cooking lessons. Before I knew it, I had my own denomination."
Mike: "Wow . . .so *that's* how religion spreads."[1]

With opinion polls, marketing savvy, and entrepreneurial enthusiasm, the church could identify felt needs, give people exactly what they wanted, and attract a large crowd of satisfied consumers. There was nothing wrong with the church that programmatic pragmatism couldn't fix.

## The Church: It Is All about Jesus

Neither the Religion of Big Ideas, nor the Religion of Big Causes, nor the Religion of the Big Deal transformed the church. What's more, they left me empty and frustrated. I sensed that in pursuit of those religions, I was being unfaithful to my calling. What I came to realize was that the church and I could be thinking Big Ideas, working on Big Causes, and pursuing the Big Deal and have nothing to do with Jesus Christ. I could be an intellectual, an activist, or an entrepreneur and not be a disciple, a follower, of Jesus. And—I know I risk sounding simplistic here—without Jesus, why bother?

I have probably already been misunderstood, so let me try to make some distinctions. Ideas matter, and I am convinced that we are called to serve and love God with our minds. Christianity is not about pretending that a lot of things that aren't true are true. The church benefits from the faithful labors of its people, in every intellectual discipline, who rigorously pursue the truth. Nonetheless, for the Christian, the life of the mind is ultimately dedicated to God as God has been revealed in Jesus Christ. I take Jesus seriously when he says, "If you continue in my word, you are truly my disciples; and you will know the truth, and the truth will make you free" (John 8:32); and "I am the way, and the truth, and the life" (John 14:6). By means of commitment to Jesus Christ and his word, our minds are shaped and tutored for the freedom that comes from an encounter with truth. Ideas matter, and their significance and weight are known fully by those people who think with minds taught by Christ.

Justice, peace, and human dignity are causes that matter; and I know that we are called to be makers of peace, shapers of justice, and workers of mercy. The reign of God is that state of life in which all things and all people are brought into shalom—wholeness, rest, and peace—and we have a mandate to pray and labor for the coming of the reign "on earth as it is in heaven." The issue in all activism is motivation. If our motives for compassionate activism are rooted in idealism, then we will be discouraged when the problems do not yield quickly to our efforts. If we believe that everyone who is attracted to a good cause is a good person, then we will be disillusioned when we discover that all people, including ourselves, are capable of self-ishness, prejudice, and even corruption. Workers for justice are not immune to the temptations of cynicism and opportunism; neither are they insured against disappointment and frustration. The motive for activism needs, therefore, to be obedience to and partnership with Jesus.

In company with Jesus, we find the holiness that challenges and purifies our own motives, the grace that accepts our weaknesses and forgives our failures, and the courage to persevere in the face of trouble. Justice, peace, and human dignity matter; but it is Jesus, and his vision of the reign of God, who inspires and energizes our work. Not idealism and not ideology, but Jesus!

Meeting human needs matters, and I am certain that our response to people's wounds and questions is an important part of the church's ministry. How, though, do we know people's real and deep needs? Are we to equate feelings of discomfort, or of desire, with needs? Is something a need just because we want it and do not have it? Or because we don't want it, but can't get rid of it? Surveys and focus groups can help us know what people are struggling with and look-ing for, but they do not describe the most fundamental needs of a human being.

From the perspective of the Christian faith, we do not know fully who we are meant to be or what our needs are until we meet Jesus Christ. Jesus is the bread for the deepest kind of hunger, water for the most basic thirst, and light for the most impenetrable darkness. Jesus does not meet the needs we think we have; instead he reveals and meets our true needs. The needs of people matter, but humanity's most real needs cannot be ascertained by opinion poll or met by savvy marketing. What is required is an encounter with Jesus.

Ideas matter; the causes of justice, peace, and dignity matter. Because these things matter, Jesus matters most of all. The church does not exist to serve the Religion of the Big Anything; instead it exists to love, serve, and make known Jesus Christ.

When Paul wrote to the church in Corinth, it was, as all churches are to some degree, troubled. There was a strain of immaturity that was manifested in jealousy and quarreling and rooted in selfishness (what Paul calls "the flesh"; see 1 Cor 3:1-5). The church was fractured into factions, some claiming allegiance to one leader and others to another: "I belong to Apollos" or "I belong to Paul."

To counter the confusion and conflict, Paul compared the church to "God's field" and "God's building." If we think of the church as God's field, then its leaders are farmhands—some plant, some water—but credit for anything that grows in that field belongs to the only power that can cause life to grow up out of the dust of the earth: "So neither the one who plants nor the one who waters is anything, but only God who gives the growth" (1 Cor 3:7). There is, Paul maintained, no good reason for jealousy and rivalry based on loyalty to particular leaders; they are all servants who depend on God for anything productive that happens.

One of the troubles with the Religions of the Big Idea, the Big Cause, and the Big Deal are that they inflame the egos of leaders and allow them to forget that they are servants and not masters. I must confess that one of the attractions of the *Big Religions* is the opportunity they give leaders to think of themselves as *big shots*. Unfortunately, I know these things not just from reading but from painful experience. Big Religions with big shot leaders crowd out the awareness that the church belongs to God and that its vitality depends finally on God. Paul urged the Corinthians not to forget that the church was God's field.

Then Paul compared the church to a building. A strong and secure foundation has been put in place; "No one can lay any foundation other than the one that has been laid; that foundation is Jesus Christ" (1 Cor 3:11). Paul urged church leaders to take care of how they built on that foundation. Some church leaders would do so wisely, some foolishly; and the final word on what is worthwhile belongs to God:

> The work of each builder will become visible, for the Day [of Judgment] will disclose it, because it will be revealed with fire, and the fire will test what sort of work each has done. (1 Cor 3:13)

There is warning in these words: in every generation the church risks building its life in ways that are out of character with the gospel of Jesus Christ. There is hope in these words: the church belongs to God, and God will not ultimately allow anything that is inconsistent with Jesus Christ to stand.

So, I hope you do not think me naive or simplistic when I claim: the church is all about Jesus. The noted theologian Jürgen Moltmann in his compelling study entitled *The Church in the Power of the Holy Spirit* made the same point, only more elegantly:

Christ is his church's foundation, its power and its hope. . . . Every statement about the church will be a statement about Christ. . . . The church's first and most significant word is not "church" but "Christ." . . . Christ is the starting point in the church's own self-understanding. . . . The church is the fellowship of those who owe their new life and hope to the activity of the risen Christ.[2]

The church! It really is all about Jesus.

## The Church: Implications of the Christ Claim

So what are the implications of this claim that the church is all about Jesus? Here are three.

(1) We become members of the church by making a commitment to Jesus Christ. In the Baptist vision, the church is a fellowship of the redeemed; one of our distinctives is our insistence on a *regenerate church membership*. For us, we are in the church because we are *in Christ*. While the church has sociological characteristics in common with voluntary associations, clubs, and social groups, the church is other and more than these. The Church is the *Company of the Committed*[3]—people who have pledged their lives to a lifelong following of Jesus Christ.

(2) The church orders its life according to the will of Christ. In practical and functional terms, Baptist churches function as democracies: free debate; one member, one vote; and majority rule. Actually, the point of church democracy is to guard against the church's being ruled by one—a monarchy—or ruled by a few—oligarchy. Our goal is to become a *Christocracy* in which we are governed by Jesus Christ.[4] We are not here, strictly speaking, to do what pleases us; we are here to please and honor Christ.

(3) The surest way to strengthen a church is by strengthening the relationship of its members with Jesus Christ. People who have a vibrant, growing, and loving relationship with Jesus Christ will be tools Christ can use in the building of a vibrant, growing, and loving church. The best thing you and I could do for our churches—indeed, for the world—is to rediscover our love for, and commitment to, Jesus.

I dream of a church that engages the mind, bringing the best of our thinking into the service of Christ; of a church that uses our strength and compassion, laboring alongside Jesus for justice and peace; and of a church that touches the heart, joining Jesus in meeting the crying needs of desperate people. I dream of the day when, as people make contact with our churches, they come to know, love, and follow Jesus Christ. He is what church is all about.

# Notes

[1]G. B. Trudeau, *Doonesbury*, Universal Press Syndicate, 1993, 5-19.

[2]Jürgen Moltmann, *The Church in the Power of the Holy Spirit: A Contribution to Messianic Ecclesiology* (New York: Harper & Row, 1977; issued in German in 1975) 5, 6, 19, 68, 105.

[3]The title of one of D. Elton Trueblood's books (New York: Harper & Row, 1961).

[4]See P. T. Forsyth, *The Church and the Sacraments* (London: Independent Press, 1917) 12-15, 63.

# Charmers, Baptist Blood, and Soul Freedom

## *Margaret B. Hess*

As in all the churches of the saints, women should be silent in the churches. For they are not permitted to speak, but should be subordinate, as the law also says. If there is anything they desire to know, let them ask their husbands at home. For it is shameful for a woman to speak in church. Or did the word of God originate with you? Or are you the only ones it has reached? (1 Cor 14:33b-36)

I live under the deep and abiding suspicion that if you scratched me, I would bleed Baptist. And it is only because I know better that I do not come right out and say that I was born Baptist. By definition, you can't be *born* a Baptist. Being a Baptist is something you choose, a decision you make with your wits about you, a path you walk down knowingly. Whether you call it "soul freedom" or "soul competency" or "believer's baptism," the essence of "Baptist" implies a responsive act of sheer will. So let the record show that I *chose* to become a Baptist, first Southern and then later American. I willingly slipped into the uterine waters of baptism and cast my lot with a peculiar communion of people.

But that fact does not tell the whole story. It is equally true to say that to some degree I was charmed into becoming a Baptist, beguiled and enticed by a people who lived "church" in a particular, loving way. And that was how Baptist got into my blood.

I grew up in a landscape peopled by grotesque caricatures of the religiously extreme, a strange collage of individuals who lurked around the edges of mainline Southern religion. These were the folk who could have appeared in the stories of Flannery O'Connor, had she known them, as perhaps she did, at least in her imagination. Such intriguing characters lived around the edges, and they could not help but capture my religious imagination.

These characters were not welcome in the mainline Christian churches, but they haunted us nonetheless.

—The old woman, plainly dressed in clothes outdated or poor, or both, who stood on the downtown corner in all kinds of weather, handing religious tracts to all who moved within her sensory range.

—The wild-eyed man who roamed the streets dressed in burlap, posing as John the Baptist, raging about repentance as he angrily stomped the path of righteousness.

—And always, the revivalists. Dark suited and slick haired, they urged the congregation to stand, with every eye closed and every head bowed, through one last verse of "Just As I Am," while we waited, in vain, for one more recalcitrant sinner to raise a hand in admission that they were standing in the need of the blood of Jesus. In spite of the fact that I had gone forward during a Christmas Eve service in my own church, and had been baptized shortly thereafter at the tender age of twelve, my hand would always rise up, involuntarily powered by some mysterious force beyond my control. Or my repentant legs would propel me down the aisle to kneel at the altar rail to pray, one more time, to be saved, just in case. Saved from what I was never quite sure. When all was said and done, I'd been saved more times than beef stew.

This was the strange religious climate of my youth, always a wordless conviction of guilt and shame hovering in the very air that we breathed, accentuated by the bizarre and reinforced by standard issue revival preaching. In this context, it was the Baptists who provided the anchor that I needed and the map offering direction for this soul born with a hankering for God in her bones. With such intense competition for the religious imagination, the Baptists had to be downright charming to secure me as one of their own.

Church, from my early childhood, was a study in the creation and maintenance of an atmosphere where the tenuous balance of soul freedom could be lived out in community. Soul freedom, to my understanding, asserts that each individual has both the right and the responsibility to develop and sustain a relationship with God based on his/her conclusions about what scripture and tradition have to say on matters of the soul.

Goaded into self-definition by the religious extremes all around us, the Baptist church became the place where I learned the practice of holding opposites in creative tension. The Baptists gave me the hope that there were many ways to come to relationship with God, even if the revivalists might have told me otherwise. For amongst Baptists I experienced the possibility of a variety of ways to live a faithful life. In time, I saw that the Baptists rarely agreed with one another about this subject of theology. But in principle, at least, I was taught that Baptists could tolerate differences of opinion.

Living this Baptist ideal of soul freedom out in the flesh-and-bone human community is rarely an easy matter. It is mainly in retrospect that I realize that love was the primary ingredient that allowed the church to be faithful, to one degree or another, to its call to be a place where diversity could be tolerated. Diversity is both the rich soil out of which soul freedom grows and the sweet flower of such freedom.

I learned about soul freedom through my personal experience of the Baptist church, with all its contradictions and human foibles. I can speak best of my ideal of church as the place where diversity is not only tolerated but cultivated by telling my story. The crucible of learning, for me, was around the issue of the ordination of women.

From the time I was a baby, I was taught that I was to give my life to Jesus, and follow where he leads. And yet there was another, more subtle contradiction present that did not emerge until I discovered that I felt called to preach the gospel. "Oh, I guess we didn't mention the one exception to following where Jesus leads." The prohibitions against women preaching were more clearly stated in some Baptist churches than in my home church, but the hesitancy to affirm the call of women to ordained ministry was present nonetheless.

As my call began to emerge, I intuited that a discussion around the issue would not be welcomed in my home church. I was not completely wrong about that, but neither was I fully correct in my assessment. Tentatively, I approached the associate pastor of my home church in 1979, informing him that I had fled to a northern seminary under the cover of night, and that I was considering pastoral ministry. When he laughed, it was not an unkind laugh, but a realistic laugh that reflected an awareness of the storm clouds gathering on the horizon of our denomination. The ordination of women would be a difficult issue as a Southern Baptist, this much I knew to be true. But I had something more to learn about the power of love in a congregation to transcend the differences of opinion on that issue. Soul freedom looked good in print, but living it out required a resiliency we had yet to test.

I agonized over the mixed messages. There was much to support the internal call that was growing in my life, and yet without the conferred authority of the church, the inner call could not stand. Then an

interesting parallel process of transformation began to occur. In my
inner life, it was marked by the beginning of the dreams about
preaching. They were the usual anxiety dreams a preacher has about
feeling unprepared or uncertain. But one dream stood out in
particular.

In that dream, I was to preach in my home church. I stood in front
of a full congregation. I had no sermon, no text, no notes, and no idea
of what I was supposed to say. I was terrified. But one thing gave me
courage. The man who had introduced me to the congregation had
taken his seat on the front row. He leaned forward, eager anticipation
written all over his face. Everything about his posture, expression, and
body language said to me: "Go ahead Meg, you have something to
say." The man in the dream was Dr. L. D. Johnson. In waking life, he
had been the pastor of my church when I was on the cradle roll. He
had dedicated me to God when I was an infant. The dream was a
clear internal message calling me to move in a direction I had not
anticipated, and encouraging me to find my voice as a preacher.

I took soul freedom seriously; it led me to find my own way in
biblical interpretation and assessing God's call in my life. But what
about the church? Could they tolerate my very different interpretation
of scripture tradition? Would there be the space for the acceptance of
the authority of my experience? There were many indications that the
answer would be no.

But an external transformation was taking place in the life of my
church. The women were at work behind the scenes, I am sure of it,
working to create an invitation for me to preach. The interim pastor
courageously raised the issue of asking me to come as a guest
preacher. And finally the day came when the chair of the deacons
called and said: "Will you come and speak to us on Sunday morning
when you are home for vacation?" "Let me clarify," I said. "Do you
want me to come and speak, or preach?" Preach it was.

The day I finally stepped into the pulpit in my home church was
a day of terror and joy. What if women really *were* to remain silent in
church, as many had told me? What if the apostle Paul was right?
What if God smites me mute? By the gracious presence of God I was
able to preach, my very presence bearing testimony to the power of
soul freedom, the latitude for believers to interpret the faith in different ways, and to live it out in the context of a community where
we do not always agree. Oddly enough, the associate pastor I had
spoken to the year before was in the congregation that day. He had
left the church, but happened to be back visiting. He came up to me

following the service and said, "God will have a place for you to preach."

Baptists cannot help but disagree with one another; it is in our nature to do so. But the ongoing question that plagues us still has to do with whether we can be held by the bonds of love in a way that allows us to disagree with grace and humility. For what is love but the commitment to the growth and development of another? I am convinced that it was the love of my Sunday School teachers and pastors and friends in that church that sustained me enough to argue with the tradition.

I know there were many who did not believe in women in the pulpit, but they were there to listen, and to be open to a new possibility. I also know that many women have experienced terrible rejection and pain at the hands of churches where they were loved into being as children. Yet I sense that it was the power and presence of love in that church, as human as it was, that helped me to become more fully who God called me to be through the acceptance of my gifts and call.

Each Sunday, I stand in front of my American Baptist congregation amazed at the diversity present. White, African-American, Hispanic, Romanian—we are a diverse ethnic and cultural mix of people. Old and young, straight and gay, well-off and poor—we reflect a variety of orientations and lifestyles. Also present is theological diversity, for there is room for different perspectives in faith.

Maintaining a supportive climate for such diversity is a challenge. At times we find it painful to disagree. But there is a growing sense that this is what it means to be church, to be Baptist. For God calls us to be about the hard work of defining who we are and where we stand, and at the same time to be open to the other being in a different place. I cannot help but fear for the future of the Baptists; for, sadly, what they proclaim best, soul freedom, is often what they do poorly. Living their espoused theology with integrity is the central challenge to all Baptists today. Clearly, a community that can sustain soul freedom can only be created through love that values the growth and life of the other as much as of the self. The issue is as much relational as it is theological.

I still visit my home church in Danville, Virginia, the place where I first learned about the possibility of a church rooted in soul freedom. I see the ways that they have both failed and succeeded to live out the diversity of such freedom in their long history. Where they have succeeded in modeling the capacity to be open to diversity, where they have been able to flourish as people with differences in genuine relationship with one another, I see the presence of love. I often think of the ones whose love made it possible for me to claim my gifts for ministry. I still see their faces and hear their voices and feel their touch, saints both living and dead.

One of the last times I preached there, I remember looking out at the congregation and seeing Sally Soyars sitting there. Sally seemed old when I was young. I first knew her when I was in the nursery, and she would come and hover over the "babies" as she called us. Sally was a real charmer. When I was five years-old, I brought Miss Sally a small seashell from our trip to the beach. She always reminded me that she had kept that seashell. I often wondered what it was like for Miss Sally to see a woman in the pulpit. Did it fit with her theology? How did she reconcile what she had always been taught with this unexpected development?

The last time I saw Sally, she sat in the congregation as I preached. The seat next to her was empty. Her husband, Gene, had died unexpectedly the year before. She had not been well; you could see that in her haunted eyes and paper thin, pale skin. Sally sat on the edge of her pew, looking like a fragile teacup about to break. Following the service, she came up to me, and slipped her frail, old, hand into mine. And in a tremulous voice, sounding like the voice of someone who had not spoken in a long time, she said: "I'm so proud of my girl. I've still got that seashell you gave me." And that is precisely why if you scratch me, I will bleed Baptist.

# Church Membership
# What Does It Mean?
# What Can It Mean?

## *Alan Neely*

O Lord God of hosts, hear my prayer; give ear, O God of Jacob! Behold our shield, O God; look on the face of your anointed. For a day in your courts is better than a thousand elsewhere. I would rather be a door-keeper in the house of my God than live in the tents of wickedness. For the Lord God is a sun and shield; he bestows favor and honor. No good thing does the Lord withhold from those who walk uprightly. O Lord of hosts, happy is everyone who trusts in you. (Ps 84:8-12)

For just as the body is one and has many members, and all the members of the body, though many, are one body, so it is with Christ. For in the one spirit we were all baptized into one body—Jews or Greeks, slaves or free—and we were all made to drink of one Spirit.

Indeed, the body does not consist of one member but of many. If the foot would say, "Because I am not a hand, I do not belong to the body," that would not make it any less a part of the body. And if the ear would say, "Because I am not an eye, I do not belong to the body," that would not make it any less a part of the body. If the whole body were an eye, where would the hearing be? If the whole body were hearing, where would the sense of smell be? But as it is, God arranged the members in the body, each one of them, as he chose. If all were a single member, where would the body be? As it is, there are many members, yet one body. The eye cannot say to the hand, "I have no need of you," nor again the head to the feet, "I have no need of you." On the contrary, the members of the body that seem to be weaker are indispensable, and those members of the body that we think less honorable we clothe with greater honor, and our less respectable members are treated with greater respect; whereas our more respectable members do not need this. But God has so arranged the body, giving the greater honor to the inferior member, that there may be no dissension within the body, but the members may have the same care for one another. If one member suffers, all suffer together with it; if one member is honored, all rejoice together with it.

Now you are the body of Christ and individually members of it. (1 Cor 12:12-27)

*[One factor that provoked Baptists to separate from the predominant Protestant bodies in the sixteenth and seventeenth centuries was the conviction of our forebears that the church should be composed not of everyone, but of believers, regenerated members. Reflecting on this early history, I begin my classes in Baptist polity at Princeton Seminary by asking two questions: (1) Given our historic emphasis on believer's baptism, are we Baptists today producing any more believers than say the Methodists, Presbyterians, or Roman Catholics? (2) Are we producing better, that is, more committed believers? The questions are meant to be rhetorical, but inevitably they engender much debate.*

*Insistence on the baptism only of believers made sense in the context of fifteenth- and sixteenth-century Europe. It made a difference. Does it make a difference today? I am not sure it does. It seems to me, therefore, that the place to begin rethinking how to generate vitality in Baptist churches is to rethink the meaning of membership. Thus the following sermon.]*

*****

"How big is your church?" Have you ever been asked that question? What does the question imply? What does the questioner want to know? The size of the sanctuary or how many names are on the church role? It could be either, but likely it is the latter. It is a common question because a conventional standard for measuring the strength and vitality of a congregation is the number of members.

This is certainly true among Baptists. Associations, state conventions, and national conventions all report annually these figures. So do the Cooperative Baptist Fellowship and the Alliance of Baptists. Dr. George Gallup and his organization in Princeton conduct regular surveys on the state of the churches in the U.S., and the data collected invariably include as a major component the *number* of people in our country who are members of the churches and synagogues.

## Churches Customarily Are Judged by the Size of the Membership

Membership size is not the only standard, of course, but it is a principal, if not *the* principal measure. Most congregations are, to an extent, concerned about the number of members they have, and assign to someone—the church clerk, for example—the task of keeping the roll or list of members accurate and up-to-date.

In most congregations it is also considered important that the *number of members* increase, or, failing this, that the total at least not diminish. We Baptists have developed an astute system by which we maintain two church rolls. What is that system? We have what are called *resident* and *non-resident* members. The irony occasionally observed is that some non-resident members often attend more frequently and support the church more generously than many of the resident members.

The Methodists, meanwhile, also have two lists: one of *active* and another of *inactive* church members. To be considered active, a Methodist must attend a minimum of four times a year.

Pastors are routinely evaluated by the number of members they add to the church roll. Moreover, if a pastor moves from one congregation to another, we have come to expect that the new congregation will be larger, that is, have *more* members. I will tell you a professional secret. Pastors infrequently—almost never in fact—accept calls to congregations that are smaller than the congregations they are serving. This is true, not only among Baptists, but across the board. Whether they are Methodist, Presbyterian, United Church of Christ, Episcopalian, or Roman Catholic, when pastors move, they expect and are expected to go to larger churches. And when in very rare cases a pastor or priest goes (or is assigned) to a smaller parish, eyebrows are raised and questions are asked. "Why would he or she go to a *smaller* church?"—smaller meaning, of course, one with less members.

## Recovering the New Testament Meaning of Being a Member of Christ's Body, the Church

Well over half the New Testament consists of letters to and information about various first-century congregations. My guess is that we have more concrete, inside information about the church at Corinth than we have about our own church. Yet, the New Testament never gives what we now consider *the vital statistics* about any church, for example, the number of members, the amount of the budget, or how many additional members they gained or how many they lost in a given period of time. Why? Because this kind of information was not considered vital.

Counting members and maintaining lists of names and addresses is a relatively recent innovation that apparently began in the sixteenth century after the Reformation and became an increasingly frequent practice in the seventeenth, eighteenth, and nineteenth centuries as a means of determining who should be admitted to the Lord's table, that is, to communion. Few denominations today do not keep this information, but they keep the lists now for different reasons.

In medieval Europe virtually everyone, other than Jews, was considered a Christian, and therefore *everyone* was a member of the church. There was no need to keep a church roll. Lists were kept only of those who were *not* permitted to receive the sacraments. This was largely true of the Roman Catholic Church in Colombia, South America, when my wife and I went there as missionaries in 1964.

Referring to Christ's disciples as members occurs rarely in the entire New Testament, once in the apostle Paul's first letter to the church in Corinth, chapter 12, verses 12-27.

## What Did the Apostle Mean by the Term "Member"?

To determine Paul's meaning of "member," we need to recognize that his language is metaphorical. And what is a metaphor? It is a figure of speech, for example,

- "He is as thin as a rail."
- "She is the salt of the earth."
- "He is as honest as the day is long."
- "She is as pretty as a picture."
- "He is as mean as a snake."
- "He is as clean as a whistle (or a hound's tooth)."
- "She is as pure as new driven snow."

All these expressions are examples of metaphorical language. The person about whom the metaphor is used is clearly not a rail, salt, picture, snake, whistle, or newly driven snow. Neither is the Apostle saying that Christ's disciples in the first century were literally, that is physically, the various parts of Christ's body. The same can be said of the bread and the wine of communion. They are not materially or substantively the body and blood of Christ.

Paul's use of the term members is also mystical or theological language. Theological language is not untrue. In fact, it reflects and reveals deeper truth. Neither is metaphorical language untrue or less true because it is a figure of speech. Both metaphorical and theological language are more graphic, for they stimulate the imagination more than simply stating something in a matter-of-fact, concrete sense. Though metaphorical expressions, such as those already mentioned, are not to be taken literally, they do reflect and communicate a reality. In the same way, mystical or theological language reflects a deeper truth than language that is scientifically or literally precise. Theological language, nonetheless, must be interpreted.

It is crucial that we note that Paul does not say to the group of disciples in Corinth, "You are members of the First Christian Church of Corinth." Rather he declares, "You are members of the body of Christ." What does he mean? He obviously is not referring to a membership list. He is talking about something much more decisive, much more profound, much more consequential. He elaborates:

— You are members or parts of a single body, the same body (v. 12).
— All of you, whether you are Jew, Greek, or whatever, "were all baptized into one body and you were made to drink of one Spirit" (v. 13). No ritual or rite so exemplifies our equality as the rite of baptism. It signifies our *sameness* and our *oneness*.
— This body of Christ is not a single organ, but a carefully arranged unit of several members or body parts (vv. 14, 17-19).
— There are no inferior parts, and there are no dispensable parts. To function properly, all the parts are needed and equally indispensable (vv. 15-16, 20-24).
— No part can function independently of the others. To function as intended, each body part has to function in harmony with the others; that is, the parts have to work together.
— If one part is sick, diseased, or hurting, the whole body is affected (v. 26).
— This is the way God has created the body "so that there may be no dissension within the body, [and that] the members may have the same care for one another" (v. 25).

To be a member of Christ's body in the first century, that is, to be a part of the church, the Apostle declared, one had to have and maintain a vital, living connection to Christ. No less imperative, one had to have and maintain a living, unified, working relationship with the other body parts or members.

## Employing and Applying the Language
## What "Member" Means Today

If we leave the matter here, however, we miss the point of the passage for us in this last decade of the twentieth century. To employ this Pauline term in a casual or perfunctory way can be very misleading.

But to understand and apply it can likewise be tough and risky. It can make us all feel uncomfortable, and it should prompt us to examine some longstanding traditions. I want to ask you four questions.

*Can a church really have non-resident members and be church, that is, the body of Christ?* Imagine yourself meeting a person who is missing a finger, a hand, an arm, or a leg. Likely, you will not blurt out, "What happened to your finger?" or "Where's your hand?" Moreover, I would hope you would not stare intently at the person's anatomy as if you were looking for the missing body part.

Let us suppose that after a reasonable amount of time—a week, a month, or several months—you have gotten to know the individual and now consider him or her a friend. Yet, nothing has been said by either of you about the missing finger, hand, arm, or leg. You cannot wait any longer. You have to know. So you muster up your courage and say, "How did you lose your finger?" or "How did you lose your hand?" and the individual responds, "Lose my finger? I haven't lost it. It's in California." Or, "My arm is in Tennessee," or "My leg is in Texas." The finger, arm, or leg may very well be somewhere else, but I want to tell you something: if it has been there very long, it is no longer alive. It is dead.

Body parts, to remain alive, must be attached to the body. In fact, they have no life or meaning apart from the body, the whole. Being a Christian *en solitaire*—detached, separated from the body—is simply not possible (at least not for long).

*Can a church have inactive members and be healthy and whole?* One thing we know: parts of our body not utilized, not exercised eventually become useless and a burden. The fact is, however, many Christian congregations are composed of large numbers of so-called inactive members. Carrying the example already employed one step further, imagine meeting and getting to know a person who has only one arm. Eventually you hesitantly inquire, "How did you lose your arm?" and the individual replies, "My arm? Huh, what do you know about that? I hadn't noticed it was missing." Are you aware of how many body parts are missing from your church?

In the 1960s and 70s when my wife and I were missionaries in Colombia, I received a telephone call one night about 10:00 P.M. The caller was a missionary friend of ours, Joyce Magyar. She was not crying, but she was obviously upset. She said, "Alan, can you come over? I think I've cut the end of my finger off in the door." I did not ask any questions. I simply replied, "I'll be right there." I jumped in the car and drove as fast as I could to the Magyars' home. When I arrived, the porch light was on, and the front door was standing open. I went in and found Joyce standing in the kitchen with a towel wrapped around her hand. I did not ask where her husband John was. He often traveled. But that was irrelevant at the time. I did not ask about their children, and I do not remember seeing them. The only question I asked was, "Where is the end you think you cut off?" She said she did not know. "Where did it happen?" I asked. "In the front door," she replied.

I rushed to the front door, but the hall and porch lights were too dim for me to see. So I asked Joyce for a flashlight. She pointed to one by the refrigerator. I grabbed it, went back to the front door, got down on my hands and knees, and with the flashlight began to search for the end of Joyce's finger. Finally I saw what appeared to be a small piece of cotton. I picked it up, took it into the bright light of the kitchen, and sure enough, it was the missing piece of her finger. The fact is, I had never looked for a missing body part and did not know at first what it was when I found it. I expected to see something with blood on it, but it was white, absolutely colorless, as white as snow. I wrapped it in my handkerchief, put the handkerchief in my pocket, and we headed for the hospital emergency room.

All went well until the surgeon began sewing the two parts together. I wanted to watch. I tried to watch, but I began to get sick, I mean really sick. I stumbled out into the hall, slumped down against the wall until I was sitting on the floor. I put my head between my knees to avoiding passing out completely. After a while, the procedure was over, and I went back to where the doctor was putting a bandage on Joyce's finger and hand. He gave her a tetanus shot and told her that he could not promise her that the graft would be successful. But it was successful, and today Joyce Magyar's finger, though it bears the scars, is whole and useable.

Virtually every congregation I know has missing body parts. Should we be looking for them? Will we know what they are when we see them? If we find them, what then?

*Can there be constant dissension, high levels of conflict, and the church function in a redemptive way as the body of Christ?* Paul says that God has made us one body, and to function properly, to function normally, there must be unity, not discord and dissension. At the same time, for the body to function effectively, there must be a certain degree of tension in the muscles. Tension therefore is both necessary and healthy; but tension that becomes so intense as to cause spasms is paralyzing.

Like the physical body, a church that is alive and well experiences certain healthy and necessary tensions. But when tension escalates into partisan rivalry and hostility, into fighting or bitter and divisive controversy, the body is immobilized. In times like this, a peace committee is in order. Rarely, however, and probably never should such a committee be composed of those involved in the controversy. Why? Because such individuals cannot be objective, and rather than contributing to true understanding, they will further divide the body. Someone from the outside—a consultant or consultants—is needed.

Most of us have known people who have suffered an accident or stroke that has left them partially paralyzed. For such victims to live reasonably normal lives, they often have to go through what is called rehabilitation. That is, they have to retrain their arms and/or legs to function in harmony with the rest of the body. When there are high levels of conflict or continual dissension in a church, a program of rehabilitation is needed, not amputation. Sometimes, albeit infrequently, body parts can become so diseased that healing and restoring them to usefulness is not possible. Not to amputate them risks the health and life of the whole body. But before we allow someone to cut off or excise any part, we need to be confident that the diagnosis is accurate, the surgeon is competent, and we should always seek a second opinion.[1]

*How many members does your church have, and how many do you need?* The only criterion is that you need enough to do Christ's ministry in the place where you are. In verses 28-31 of the text, Paul lists several, seven to be precise, kinds of gifts God had given to certain persons. For a church to function properly and effectively, the Apostle implied, a variety of gifts was needed: apostles, prophets, teachers, miracle workers, healers, those who spoke in tongues, and those who interpreted. These seven spiritual gifts were not offices or positions to be held as much as they were tasks to be performed. Are these seven clear-cut categories indispensable for the body to function today? Can a church function today precisely as it did in the first century?

Most of us would agree, I believe, that Christ still calls and sends individuals as his emissaries (apostles) into the world. Announcing the good news by word and deed (evangelists), doing the miraculous, healing, voicing praise and thanksgiving, and enabling the dull of hearing to understand what is happening are all needed. But note, in the First Epistle of Peter, not seven, but two gifts or functions are mentioned: the gift or ministry of the word (1:10-12) and the gift or ministry of helping (4:7-10). Even in this Corinthian letter, the spiritual gifts mentioned by the Apostle can be reduced to two: gifts given whereby one may bless others, and gifts whereby one's own life is blessed. Whatever the gift of tongues is, as far as Paul is concerned, it falls into this second category. It edifies the individual. This is not to imply that it is insignificant; but the gift of tongues does not edify the church as a whole. For this reason, Paul sets limits on its importance and use.[1]

A congregation can become so intent on reproducing the New Testament pattern of the church, ignoring the fact that nearly two millennia separate us from the first century, that the members attempt to copy, to replicate in the most minute detail what they understand the first-century church was like and what the believers did. They can refuse to use musical instruments, electric lights, or computers on the basis that these modern inventions or tools are not mentioned in the New Testament. They can scrap the contemporary terms and revert to New Testament words such as bishop, elder, and deacon— assuming, wrongly I believe, that imitating the first-century church is desirable and will assure effectiveness.

What is important, what *is* indispensable, is not the tools or the terminology we use, but our understanding of and commitment to the task we have—to be light, salt, and leaven. Ah, you readily see that light, salt, and leaven are also metaphorical and theological expressions. Interpreted, they imply that the church, if it is to be the living body of Christ, must and will penetrate and impact the culture of which it is a part.

Two years ago I received an invitation from a Mennonite Church in Goshen, Indiana, to be the guest preacher in what the members call "Renewal Month." In a letter dated November 17, 1994, the pastor explained what Renewal Month is for the congregation.

> Every three years, the membership of the church is for all practical purposes erased from the book. Then during October, every member and associate member must at some time during the month give serious attention to their relationship to Christ and the church to determine if they wish to continue in the fellowship of the church. If that is their desire, they come to the church during the daytime or early evening and write their names in a special book. Although the book is by no means the *Lamb's Book of Life*, writing their name in it does signal a renewed commitment and *puts them back on the membership roll*.

It strikes me that this pastor and congregation are moving in the right direction, for they are seeking in a straightforward, nonjudgmental, and equitable way to recover the profound but largely lost significance of what it means to be a member of the body of Christ, to be a member of the church.

## Note

[1]The test of whether a gift comes from God depends on whether it contributes to "the common good," i.e., the whole body (12:7), and whether it builds up and edifies the whole Christian community (8:1).

# Back to the Basics

## *John R. Tyler*

How very good and pleasant it is when kindred live together in unity! It is like the precious oil on the head, running down upon the beard, on the beard of Aaron, running down over the collar of his robes. It is like the dew of Hermon, which falls on the mountains of Zion. For there the Lord ordained his blessing, life forevermore. (Ps 133)

Pursue love and strive for the spiritual gifts, and especially that you may prophesy. For those who speak in a tongue do not speak to other people but to God; for nobody understands them, since they are speaking mysteries in the Spirit. On the other hand, those who prophesy speak to other people for their upbuilding and encouragement and consolation. Those who speak in a tongue build up themselves, but those who prophesy build up the church. Now I would like all of you to speak in tongues, but even more to prophesy. One who prophesies is greater than one who speaks in tongues, unless someone interprets, so that the church may be built up.

Now, brothers and sisters, if I come to you speaking in tongues, how will I benefit you unless I speak to you in some revelation or knowledge or prophecy or teaching? It is the same way with lifeless instruments that produce sound, such as the flute or the harp. If they do not give distinct notes, how will anyone know what is being played? And if the bugle gives an indistinct sound, who will get ready for battle? So with yourselves; if in a tongue you utter speech that is not intelligible, how will anyone know what is being said? For you will be speaking into the air. There are doubtless many different kinds of sounds in the world, and nothing is without sound. If then I do not know the meaning of a sound, I will be a foreigner to the speaker and speaker a foreigner to me. So with yourselves; since you are eager for spiritual gifts, strive to excel in them for building up the church.

Therefore, one who speaks in a tongue should pray for the power to interpret. For if I pray in a tongue, my spirit prays but my mind is unproductive. What should I do then? I will pray with the spirit, but I will pray with the mind also; I will sing praise with the spirit, but I will sing praise with the mind also. Otherwise, if you say a blessing with the spirit, how can anyone in the position of an outsider say the "Amen" to your thanksgiving, since the outsider does not know what you are saying? For you may give thanks well enough, but the other person is not built up. I thank God that I speak in tongues more than all of you; nevertheless, in church I would rather speak five words with my mind, in order to instruct others also, than ten thousand words in a tongue.

What should be done then, my friends? When you come together, each one has a hymn, a lesson, a revelation, a tongue, or an interpretation. Let all things be done for building up. If anyone speaks in a tongue, let there be only two or at most three, and each in turn; and let one interpret. But if there is o one to interpret, let them be silent in church and speak to themselves and to God. Let two or three prophets speak, and let the others weigh what is said. If a revelation is made to someone else sitting nearby, let the first person be silent. For you can all prophesy one by one, so that all may learn and all be encouraged. And the spirits of prophets are subject to the prophets, for God is a God not of disorder but of peace. (1 Cor 14:1-19, 26-33)

Several years ago my father (born 1903) gave me a small well-worn book entitled *Church Manual*. It had been given to him by his father (born 1859). The page that lists the publisher's name and date of publication has been lost. There is no doubt, however, that it was published by a Baptist agency, probably in the early 1900s.

The book defines the church as "either a particular congregation of the saints or the redeemed in the aggregate." All but one page of the book is devoted to the first definition, "a particular congregation of the saints" or the local church. Like the book, we give scant attention to the church that is the redeemed of the ages. It is what the Apostles' Creed calls the "holy catholic Church," the word *catholic* used here to impart its classic meaning: universal. It is what the Bible calls the Bride of Christ. But we think predominately of the church as a particular congregation of the saints. We live our Christian lives in particular congregations.

Many of us were placed on the cradle roll of a particular congregation of the saints. My godly mother had arranged months in advance for the cradle roll director to be at the hospital at my birth, hoping her newborn child might break the record for the shortest time interval between birth and entry on Central Baptist Church's cradle roll. Mind you, a record-breaking time interval was not measured in days; it was measured in hours—no, minutes!

The local church is where we cut our teeth on life. Robert L. Fulgham has written a bestselling book entitled *All I Really Need to Know I Learned in Kindergarten*. I have a slightly different twist on that. All I really need to know I learned in Sunday School departments with names such as "primaries" and "juniors" and "intermediates."

Bible sword drills gave me my first taste of refereed competition. I learned in church how to get along with other children long before I ever attended a public school. I learned about love and service to others from people such as Mrs. Wilson, our family barber's wife and the primary department director. She taught me my Sunday School lesson one Sunday morning in a car in the church parking lot. I was dressed in my pajamas because I was too sick to attend church with the other children. But I was determined to reach my goal of a year's perfect Sunday School attendance and get my perfect attendance pin. So the church came to me. That Sunday, like so many since, I did not think of the bride of Christ as meeting my needs. I saw and heard and felt Central Baptist Church meet my needs in the person of Mrs. Wilson, one of the saints who comprised its membership.

I began to learn about the opposite sex in the youth department. I often brought my dates to church services and functions. I was married in the church. I have cried and laughed and felt despair and joy and every other emotion a human can feel at church. When I die, my memorial service will be held in the church. I may be singing praises at that moment with the redeemed of the ages in heaven, but my memorial service will be in progress at a local church that has a street address and a zip code.

The local church has been my faith community, my faith family. The church looks like, acts like, walks like, and talks like a community or a family simply because it is comprised of more than one person. Church members share things in common, chief among them their confession that Jesus is Lord. They share a love for suppers, none of which is ever intended to be the last! And they share their weaknesses and their differences.

Jesus said, "Where two or three are gathered in my name, I am there among them" (Matt 18:20). He also could have said, "Where two or three are gathered in my name, there will be differences, for each of you has been created a unique personality with unique strengths and weaknesses. My Father in heaven designed it so. It is for your benefit. You'll have to trust me on this."

Perhaps the greatest benefit of living in community is its ability to strengthen and shape us. Communities and their individual members become strong by learning to deal successfully and redemptively with their diversity. All of life works this way; it's a natural law.

The man who would become stronger does not look for ways to avoid resistance; he looks for ways to encounter it and to use it to his benefit through disciplined weight training. The woman who would become a champion ice skater does not run from practice; she runs to it, practicing a set time each day for a set duration and with a particular purpose in mind at each practice session. Weight training and skating practice are not always fun. But so what? Where have we gotten this idea that everything has to be fun if we are to invest ourselves in it? It would be far better if we would ask other questions: Is it necessary? Is it profitable? Will another person be helped? Will I be a better servant for my lord?

The apostle Paul addressed questions such as these in his letters to the church at Corinth. Paul had founded this church around A.D. 52. He stayed in Corinth about eighteen months and then moved on to Ephesus. While at Ephesus, some people from the household of Chloe back at Corinth visited him and reported quarrels among the church members (1 Cor 1:11). There were several letters between Paul and the congregation. Other members at Corinth visited Paul, no doubt filling him in on all the juicy details. Paul made more than one visit to Corinth in an attempt to resolve the conflicts. What he heard and what he saw broke his heart.

No other books in the New Testament give us a better view of a local church in turmoil than do 1 and 2 Corinthians. These books are a compilation of letters Paul wrote to this congregation. Let's look at one of the problems mentioned in 1 Corinthians that was causing conflict in the church.

The members at Corinth were having difficulty handling their differences over speaking in tongues. There is no way to define "speaking in tongues" to everyone's satisfaction, but let me offer this working definition for our purpose. Speaking in tongues, as practiced at Corinth, was an ecstatic outburst of prayer and praise that was abnormal and incoherent. The speakers gave no thought to what they were uttering; conscious intellectual activity was suspended or disconnected from what was uttered. We can conclude from Paul's comments that speaking in tongues sometimes was accompanied by frenetic activity.

One can observe speaking in tongues today in churches all over the world. In fact, the phenomenon is not exclusively a Christian one. The outward manifestations vary by person, by church, by culture, by geography, and by time.

Some people find this a normal manner of expression within the church. Some find it an outrageous activity that is harmful to faith and practice. Others simply are baffled by it. But the very nature of the practice—ecstatic, unintelligible utterances sometimes accompanied by frenetic activity—guarantees there will be a difference of opinion among some groups of believers. It was a major cause of conflict and chaos among the members of First Church, Corinth.

The fourteenth chapter of 1 Corinthians discusses the matter in some detail. It is easy to view this chapter as providing an answer to these questions: Should church members speak in tongues? Is it a spiritual gift of God and, thus, a practice to be permitted and even encouraged in the church? But I want to propose that this chapter was not written to answer these questions, at least not as we usually ask them. The presence or absence of speaking in tongues was not the disease that had infected the Corinthian church. It was only a symptom of the disease. So let's watch as Paul puts on his spiritual stethoscope and examines his very sick Corinthian patient. And let's be especially watchful for his diagnosis of the disease and its cure.

Paul first contracts two kinds of utterance in church: unintelligible utterance, which he calls "speaking in tongues," and intelligible utterance, which he calls "prophesying." Prophesying means *forth*telling, not *fore*telling. It is what we call Christian preaching or teaching. I think Paul contrasts these two forms of speaking in church because he was hearing from two factions, each taking one of these positions to the exclusion of the other.

Imagine that you were in the room when Chloe's people visited Paul and told him all about the quarrels and, of course, the people doing the quarreling. Perhaps they presented both sides of the argument so Paul could get some sense of how things were going back home. Our text gives us good reason to think the conversation might have sounded something like this. Let's pretend someone named Tychicus went first.

"You wouldn't believe it, Paul. These people stand up at the most unpredictable times in the service and just say or shout pure gibberish. Nobody understands what in the world they're saying.

"How can anyone be encouraged by incoherent behavior and unintelligible speech? And Paul, they gloat. They're *sooo* proud that they have this gift—that's what they call it, a gift.

"They claim they've got the 'second blessing,' meaning, I suppose, that the rest of us are stuck back here in some second-class status. We thought we all shared one blessing: that Jesus Christ had made it possible for us to be in right relationship to God, whether slave or free, Jew or Greek, male or female.

"I invited another slave who works in a home down the street from my master's house to go with me to our worship service last Sunday. He's heard a little about Jesus but knows nothing about the gospel. And then brother Aristarchus stands up in the middle of the service and starts yelling gibberish. I'll be lucky if my friend ever speaks to me again. He thinks we're all raving lunatics. And do you know what? I think half of us are."

As Tychicus described the church's symptoms, Paul listened carefully through his spiritual stethoscope. Then someone—we'll call her Tryphena—spoke.

"That may be how Tychicus sees it, Paul, but that's not how I see it at all. He makes our speaking in tongues sound as if we're crazy people who force ourselves on others in the church. That's not true.

"You yourself said that the gospel was not a matter of lofty words and wisdom, that the power of God was in the cross, the most unlikely symbol of power in the world. And you said that God worked among us with signs and wonders so we wouldn't rely upon human power and intellect. Well Paul, those signs and wonders have come to the church through some of us. We don't understand fully what it's all about, but we know this: It is of God.

"The moving of God's spirit cannot be planned and written in advance on some order of worship. We have to utter our spiritual language when we're moved by God to do it.

"Why can't the others be glad this gift has been poured out on our church? You should hear the hall talk after church. They act as if they are the only ones who have minds capable of real intellect, as if they are the only ones able to understand the great truths of the gospel.

"I think they're jealous of the rest of us who speak in tongues. They can't or won't, so they just hide behind their little wall of intellectualism and expound on the superiority of proclamation. Well, we're not against preaching, but that doesn't mean we shouldn't be able to speak in tongues as the Spirit moves us!"

As Tryphena described the church's symptoms, Paul listened carefully through his spiritual stethoscope. Paul then promised his visitors that he'd write soon and give the church instruction on how to resolve their problems.

Paul knew he had to pray harder that night than he ever had. He would need to pray for the church members back at Corinth. He knew them all. He'd had the privilege of telling them the gospel story and of seeing them respond to it by believing that Jesus was their Lord and Savior.

He thought of his great calling from God: to declare throughout the known world that the wall between Jew and Gentile had been broken down forever by the power of God in Christ Jesus. "Imagine it," Paul thought, "people of all races and cultures and nations and backgrounds and status and wealth can now be joined together into

God's family and can build the kingdom in local churches where they live!"

He thought of a wealthy Greek woman named Phoebe sitting in church with a slave named Romulus on one side and a Jew named Sarah on the other. What a glorious sight! It was that picture of a diverse humanity saved and united by Christ that kept him going when the going got tough. And Paul said to himself, "I would never have thought it possible just a few years ago back in Jerusalem!"

And speaking of Jerusalem, there were influential Christian leaders there who were having difficulty giving up their old Jewish exclusiveness. They would say on a good day that the wall had come down between Jew and Gentile, as long as the Gentiles practiced their faith according to traditional customs, but on most days Paul knew they did not yet really believe it.

What if the church at Corinth imploded? How could the dream of God's reconciliation with a diverse humanity be kept alive if churches failed because their diverse members couldn't get along with one another?

And then Paul prayed.

"Blessed are you, O LORD our God, King of the universe. For you have broken down the barrier that not only separates humanity from you, but nation from nation and race from race.

"You have established your church that it may be a living picture of the reconciling gospel. You have said that the gates of hell shall not prevail against it. Look down, O LORD, on your church at Corinth. The gates of hell are prevailing there through the folly of the redeemed.

"The church is in disarray. Brothers and sisters are bickering and quarreling with one another. They have attached themselves and their identity to preachers (God help us all!) rather than to you and the gospel, for one says, 'I belong to Paul,' and another says 'I belong to Apollos,' and another says 'I belong to Cephas.' At least there are some who still say, 'I belong to Christ.'

"Believers are suing one another, and in the Roman courts, of all places! Some have finally learned that the gospel has freed them from petty rules, such as the prohibition to eat meat that has been offered to idols and the need for circumcision. Others have not yet learned this, but they are good people, LORD. They just haven't reached this level of understanding. Yet those who claim they have reached it haven't learned to love one another as Christ taught us.

"How can the so-called strong have completely missed Gospel 101? Why can't they learn that what is permissible is not always right because it is not always helpful? They seem always to focus their attention on their rights rather than their duties, on their freedom rather than their responsibilities.

"And now this latest mess over speaking in tongues has shaken the church to its very foundations. The attitudes of both factions, if they continue unchecked, will be fatal to your church at Corinth.

"LORD God, what is the value of tongues uttered in pride? What is the value of proclamation spoken without love? What is the use of signs and wonders if they are hidden by chaos and distrust? What is the value of intellectual pursuit if it only creates a long nose with which to look down on others?

"LORD God, hear me now. Be not silent to me! Your church at Corinth is in critical condition. As a result, your name isn't faring too well there. I badly need your help to fix this mess, and frankly, you need mine. Give me guidance to know how best to respond so that the gospel will not wither and die before its roots have taken hold. Give me the wherewithal to write a letter that will bring permanent healing. Through Jesus Christ my lord. Amen."

Paul tumbled and tossed most of the night. The next morning he called for his secretary. He began to dictate a letter to the church at Corinth.

His letter carefully avoided telling either side they were completely wrong or completely right. First of all, it's a rare case indeed when either side is completely right. And besides, you can't bring reconciliation if you take only one side's position. So Paul took the positions of both sides.

In one breath he says there's something to be said for speaking in tongues; in fact, he wishes all the Corinthians spoke in tongues. In the next breath, he begins with "But on the other hand" and speaks well for the position of those who want to exclude the speaking of tongues in church.

He says he supports anything that builds up the individual, but he states emphatically that individuals must always act in accordance with what *builds up the church*. He pleads not for individual rights but for corporate responsibility. "Since you are eager for spiritual gifts," he says, "strive to excel in them for building up the church" (1 Cor 14:12).

Paul makes room for everyone and their gifts. "What should be done then, my friends? When you come together, each one has a hymn, a lesson, a revelation, a tongue, or an interpretation. Let all things be done for building up" (1 Cor. 14:26). He gets down to particulars.

Paul says that people may speak in tongues, but only one, two or three at most, and they must do it in an orderly manner. Paul recognizes that moderation will go a long way in curing the dissension that has been created by the excesses of both factions. Paul gives freedom to speak in tongues to those who want it, but in a way that hopefully will not be disruptive to those who find it baffling.

Paul then says to let two or three (notice the equal number) prophets proclaim the gospel clearly, and let all weigh what is said; that is, let both factions now put their intellect to it (1 Cor 14:27-33). Then he closes his discussion with these words: "So, my friends, be eager to prophesy, and do not forbid speaking in tongues; but all things should be done decently and in order" (1 Cor 14:39-40).

I suggest that Paul isn't addressing the issue of speaking in tongues at all. He has a weightier issue on his mind. He's concerned with what has been lost at Corinth amidst a cacophony of quarrels.

Paul, arguably the greatest proponent of freedom in the New Testament, sees freedom as a servant. It is to be used to include people, not exclude them. He cares little about anyone's eating or not eating meat offered to idols. He cares immensely that gospel freedom be used for the good of all. That means the strong (knowledgeable) will need to help the weak (unknowledgeable) rather than become puffed up in their strength, a sure sign of Christian ignorance.

If eating meat offered to idols will cause the church to be weakened, then relax the doctrinal purity on this point and forego your rights. Think first of the church of God, not yourself. Paul always thinks first of the harmony and health of the church, and he's willing to modify—even bend—either or both sides of an issue if it will hold the church together.

It's with good reason that the great love chapter we know as 1 Corinthians 13 was part of a letter to this church.

> If I speak in the tongues of mortals [speakers of prophesy] and angels [speakers of tongues] but do not have love, I am a noisy gong or a clanging cymbal. . . . Love is patient; love is kind; love is not envious or boastful or arrogant or rude. It does not insist on its own way. (vv. 1, 4-5a)

I do not mean to imply that a church should accept any and all practices under any circumstances. In his letters to the church at

Corinth Paul cites several matters he says are to stop completely and immediately. He cuts them no slack whatsoever. There will be honest disagreement among people of goodwill on what is and is not negotiable. But it has been my experience that churches seldom suffer from an extreme squishiness; instead, they suffer far more often from an extreme rigidity.

I wouldn't have been surprised if some members at Corinth were ready to bail out rather than stay and be part of the solution to their family conflict. Too many church members are approaching their church family relationships the way too many people are approaching their marriages. They enter into these holy relationships with no commitment to permanence—with no commitment to stick it out in sickness and in health, for richer or poorer, in trouble-free church times and in troublesome church times. We shop for a church that catches our fancy. We stay until our fancy changes or until a difficult situation arises that requires some commitment and effort on our part to provide healing. Then we divorce our church because "we have found something in her that does not please us."

Paul's instructions in 1 Corinthians might be summed up this way: Stick it out. Make it work. Focus on the basics, not on all these peripheral issues. Keep it simple. Make love your first priority. Do everything to build up the church.

Vince Lombardi, the legendary coach of the Green Bay Packers for whom the Super Bowl trophy is named, called his players to a special team meeting one Monday morning after a disastrous loss the previous day. He told them they had been playing poorly for several weeks. He confessed that he'd been trying to fix things with complicated twists to the offensive and defensive formations, but to no avail. He then told them what they needed was a good refresher course on the basics. Then Coach Lombardi held up a pigskin and said, "Gentlemen, this is a football."

Paul addressed the conflicts at Corinth by holding up Christian love and the importance of their learning to live together as church. As he held them up in his letter, he said, "Brothers and sisters, this is the gospel." Paul called them back to the basics. We would do well to heed that call.

# If This Is Not a Place

## Lavonn D. Brown

When he came to Nazareth, where he had been brought up, he went to
the synagogue on the sabbath day, as was his custom. He stood up to
read, and the scroll of the prophet Isaiah was given to him. He unrolled
the scroll and found the place where it was written: "The Spirit of the
Lord is upon me, because he has anointed me to bring good news to the
poor. He has sent me to proclaim release to the captives and recovery of
sight to the blind, to let the oppressed go free, to proclaim the year of
the Lord's favor."

And he rolled up the scroll, gave it back to the attendant, and sat
down. The eyes of all in the synagogue were fixed on him. Then he
began to say to them, "Today this scripture has been fulfilled in your
hearing." All spoke well of him and were amazed at the gracious words
that came from his mouth. They said, "Is not this Joseph's son?" He said
to them, "Doubtless you will quote to me this proverb, 'Doctor, cure
yourself!' And you will say, 'Do here also in your hometown the things
that we have heard you did at Capernaum.' " And he said, "Truly I tell
you, no prophet is accepted in the prophet's hometown. But the truth is,
there were many widows in Israel in the time of Elijah, when the heaven
was shut up three years and six months, and there was a severe famine
over all the land; yet Elijah was sent to none of them except to a widow
at Zarephath in Sidon. There were also many lepers in Israel in the time
of the prophet Elisha, and none of them was cleansed except Naaman
the Syrian." When they heard this, all in the synagogue were filled with
rage. They got up, drove him out of the town, and led him to the brow
of the hill on which their town was built, so that they might hurl him off
the cliff. But he passed through the midst of them and went on his way.
(Luke 4:16-30)

Baptists use the word church to mean different things. Many people
think of church in terms of a building. It is located at the corner of
Webster and Comanche. "We are building a new church" is a clear
reference to a building. Others think of church primarily as denomination, as in, "To which church do you belong?" The expected answer
may include Presbyterian, Baptist, or Catholic. On occasion the word
church means nothing more than a service of worship, as in "Are you
going to church Sunday?" The danger is not that these concepts are
wrong. Rather, it is that they are partial and inadequate.

The mental images produced by the word church are as varied as they are partial. Choose one or more of the following: The church is
—a congregation of saints having achieved varying levels of sinless perfection
—a fellowship of sinners banded together to help each other live a better life
—a museum for collecting and preserving holy relics
—a spiritual army marching off the map with divine commands
—a house of hypocrisy where people play games with God
—a fellowship of loving concern picking up broken lives and restoring them

Ken Medema, the blind musician, often sees more than those of us with good vision. He wrote a song about the church.

> I don't need another place
> for trying to impress you
> with just how good and virtuous I am.
> I don't need another place
> for always being on top of things,
> ev'rybody knows that it's a sham.
> I don't need another place
> for always wearing smiles,
> even when it's not the way I feel.
> I don't need another place
> to mouth the same old platitudes,
> you and I both know that it's not real.

Medema is searching for a church, a message, a ministry that has a ring of the real. He goes on to ask some pertinent questions:

> If this is not a place
> where tears are understood,
> where can I go to cry?
> And if this is not a place
> where my spirit can take wings,
> where can I go to fly?
> If this is not a place
> where my questions can be asked,
> where shall I go to seek?
> And if this is not a place
> where my heart cries can be heard,
> where shall I go to speak?[1]

At its best the church is a place of mutual forgiveness and mutual concern. It should be a place where each member gives priority to the needs of others. It must be a fellowship of loving concern.[2]

## The Concept of the Church in the New Testament

Baptists are a people of the Book. Our first question is, "What does the Bible have to say?" Specifically, what does the New Testament say about the church?

The word church is used in the New Testament with a twofold meaning. In some instances, it refers to the whole body of believers, the fellowship of the redeemed everywhere, the people of God assembled or unassembled. In most cases, however, church refers to a local congregation. So, the Lord Jesus is head of the church composed of all true believers. At the same time, Christians are to associate themselves into particular local congregations of churches. Therefore, local congregations share the nature of the body of Christ.

What did Jesus mean by *ekklesia* (church)? At the time of Peter's great confession, Jesus said, "And on this rock I will build my church" (Matt 16:18). Later, while discussing church discipline, he said, "If the member refuses to listen to them, tell it to the church" (Matt 18:17). The word church literally means the called-out ones or those who have been summoned together. When Jesus used the word church, he was referring to a group of people whom he had called to be with him in special relationship. Early Christians first used the word to describe simple meetings and later to describe local congregations.

Paul S. Minear in his *Images of the Church in the New Testament* lists ninety-six terms used to describe the church in the New Testament. Three of these analogies help us understand the special relationship of the church to God as Father, Son, and Holy Spirit.

The church in its relationship to God the Father is described as *the people of God*. In the Old Testament, the Israelites were the people of God. The early Christian community saw itself as a continuation of the new Israel to evangelize all nations. This concept placed the New Testament church in the setting of the long story of God's dealing with the chosen people. The people of God may be the best term to describe the nature of the New Testament church.

Peter described the exiles of the Dispersion (1 Pet 1:1) this way:

But you are a chosen race, a royal priesthood, a holy nation, God's own people, in order that you may proclaim the mighty acts of him who

called you out of darkness into his marvelous light. Once you were not
a people but now you are God's people; once you had not received
mercy, but now you have received mercy. (1 Pet 2:9-10)

The church is essentially a people, a religious society. It is not a
building, but the believers themselves. The claim to be the people of
God is not an arbitrary claim to special privilege. It should not lead
to pride but to repentance. The church is the people of God only
because God dwells within and moves among God's people.

As the people of God, the church must embody the good news in
everyday life. Since God has forgiven, the people of God must forgive.
Since God has loved, the people of God must love. The people of God
must forever be a missionary and evangelizing people, taking the
gospel to all people and nations.

The church in its relationship to God the Son is best understood
in Paul's metaphor of *the body of Christ.* Paul spoke out of conviction
when he said to the Corinthians, "Now you are the body of Christ
and individually members of it" (1 Cor 12:27). The concept has
tremendous potential.

Unity in diversity is the best we can hope for in the church. Paul
wanted us to understand that "just as the body is one [unity], and has
many members [diversity], and all the members of the body, though
many [diversity], are one body [unity], so it is with Christ. Indeed, the
body does not consist of one member [unity], but of many [diversity]"
(1 Cor 12:12, 14).

In the New Testament, Christ and the church were inseparable
realities. To continue his work on earth, Christ did not leave merely
changed, isolated individuals. He left a body of believers, the church.
To think of Christ is necessarily to think of the church. To think of the
church is necessarily to think of Christ. The work of the church is
Christ's work. Through the church, his purposes are carried out in the
world.          .

In the church, each person is not only a member of the body of
Christ but also a member of all the other Christians who make up the
body. Paul wrote,

> For as in one body we have many members, and not all the members
> have the same function, so we, who are many, are one body in Christ,
> and individually we are members of one another. (Rom 12:4-5)

The members are so bound together that each person feels keenly the hurts, sorrows, and joys that come to the rest of the family. Paul urged

> that there may be no dissension within the body, but the members may have the same care for one another. If one member suffers, all suffer together with it; if one member is honored, all rejoice together with it. (1 Cor 12:25-26)

The head of the body is Christ. Paul reminded the Colossians: "He is the head of the body, the church; he is the beginning, the firstborn from the dead, so that he might come to have first place in everything" (1:18). The church is a new creation in him, and it partakes of the very life of Christ. The church's reason for being is to minister to the world as Christ's agent.

The church in its relationship to God the Holy Spirit is identified as *the fellowship of the Spirit*. In fact, the church cannot be understood apart from the person and work of the Holy Spirit. The book in the New Testament called *The Acts of the Apostles* may be more accurately named *The Acts of the Holy Spirit*.

On the day of Pentecost, the Holy Spirit manifested itself in people's lives as a transforming power. The Holy Spirit is best understood as the living presence of the risen Christ. One of the favorite descriptions of the church in the New Testament was fellowship (*koinonia*). Paul closed his letter to the Corinthian church with the familiar benediction referring to "the communion of the Holy Spirit" (2 Cor 13:13). This fellowship of loving concern was a product of the Spirit's presence.[3]

## Jesus' Ministry and the Nature of the Church

The nature of the church is best revealed in Jesus' understanding of his own ministry. Our biblical text gives good insight into Jesus' understanding of what he had come to do. Luke 4:14-15 gives a general account of the beginning of Jesus' Galilean ministry:

> Then Jesus, filled with the power of the Spirit returned to Galilee, and a report about him spread through all the surrounding country. He began to teach in their synagogues and was praised by everyone.

Clearly, Jesus used the synagogues for his teaching and work. Why?

The synagogue was Israel's supreme contribution to the history of religion. When Israel was led away captive into strange lands, there was no temple or holy place. Where would they worship and sing the Lord's songs? The answer was the local synagogue, the meeting place of Jewish worshipers.

Synagogue worship consisted of an affirmation of faith (the Shema), prayers, singing of praises, the reading of fixed selections from the law (the Torah), free selections from the prophets, an explanation or application of both, and a closing blessing by a priest or a prayer by a layman. The form of synagogue worship had a profound influence on worship in the New Testament churches. Our Christian worship is built on that foundation.

When Jesus returned to his hometown of Nazareth, "he went to the synagogue on the sabbath day, as was his custom" (Luke 4:16). Why would he do that? After all, Nazareth was a small town. The people were ordinary. The services weren't particularly inspiring. The leaders were nothing extra. Besides, he didn't agree with all that was going on. Could it be that Jesus recognized there were times, places, and associations that make the approach of God more sure? Is it possible that, in the fellowship of worship, the Spirit may kindle a fire?

At the appropriate time in worship Jesus was handed a roll of the prophet Isaiah and invited to read a selection of his choosing. He selected what we now know as Isaiah 61:1-2, which describes the work of the Messiah. Obviously, it was intended to be a description of the ministry he himself would fulfill. He began reading,

"The Spirit of the Lord is upon me. . . . " The Spirit came upon him at his baptism.

"Because he has anointed me to bring good news to the poor. . . " His ministry would be armed with the power of the Holy Spirit. He would preach, not merely to the poor in material things, but also the poor in spirit.

"To proclaim release to the captives. . . . " He would preach to those in moral and spiritual captivity. Some know of their captivity. Others do not. Still others love it. He offers deliverance to all.

"And the recovery of sight to the blind. . . . " He would offer sight to the physically and morally blind, even to those who have eyes with which to see but do not. He promises, "You will see again."

"To let the oppressed go free. . . . " His preaching would reach out to the vast audience of untouchables: the bruised, downtrodden, broken, crushed, and shattered.

"To proclaim the year of the Lord's favor." He preached in an era of grace between his first and second coming. The year of the Lord would be a time when all people would have opportunity to find acceptance with the Lord.

Then, he rolled up the scroll, gave it back to the attendant. All eyes were riveted on him, and he began to explain, "Today this scripture has been fulfilled in your hearing" (v. 21). This is Jesus' understanding of his own ministry. It instructs our understanding of the church.

## Models for the Church Today

Finally, it is essential that we understand the function of the church in contemporary society. "Let the church be the church" is an oft-heard plea. Wonderful. We all agree. But, when we let the church be the church, what will we let it be? At this point Jesus' understanding of his ministry and Ken Medema's vision of the church point us in one direction.

First, is not the church a place where our tears are understood and our heart cries heard? Jesus launched his mission by referring to that majestic passage in Isaiah 61:1, "He has sent me to bring good news to the oppressed, to bind up the brokenhearted." The psalmist's invitation was "Cast your burden on the Lord, and he will sustain you" (55:22).

A fellow minister was emerging from a series of bad experiences. He said to a group of ministers, "Dig deep enough, and you will find hurt." Our hurts and sorrows are of many kinds and multiply rapidly: broken homes, broken relationships, broken hearts, loss of health, death of a mate, loss of a friend, loss of a job, or abandonment by someone we love. Sorrow, sadness, and grief are the price we pay for loving.

In ministering to these needs, the church must enter the real world where people live. So God calls the church to love the world as it is, not as the church might wish it to be. We don't need another place for trying to impress each other, for pretending always to be on top of things, for wearing paste-on smiles, or for mouthing the same old platitudes. Rather, we need a place where tears are understood and heart cries heard.

Second, is not the church a place where our spirits can take wings? Jesus said the Spirit of the Lord had set him apart "to proclaim release to the captives." In the church should we not be encouraged to explore the heights of Christian experience? As Christians we often live in unbelievable captivity. We have learned to ride herd on our hearts, to keep from getting carried away, never to abandon ourselves to anything, and certainly not to explore the outer limits of our Christian experience.

Jesus' invitation is "Come to me, all you that are weary and are carrying heavy burdens, and I will give you rest" (Matt 11:28). He spoke to those who labor to do the works of the law and are weighed down by endless rules and regulations. To those in bondage to a religion that had become a burden, he had come to preach liberty and deliverance.

With a burst of spiritual insight Isaiah wrote,

> But those who wait for the Lord shall renew their strength, they shall mount up with wings like eagles, they shall run and not be weary, they shall walk and not faint. (Isa 40:31)

God provides the strength for exploring new heights and soaring above the obstacles. However, we do well to remember the warning that, when you desire to spread your wings and fly, there always will be those around attempting to stand on your wings.

Again, Jesus might say we don't need another place where religion has become a burden, where people are exhausted in their search for truth, where weary people go through the motions or are bound by ceremonial obedience. Rather, we need a place where our spirits can take wings, and captives are set free.

Third, is not the church a place where our questions can be asked? Jesus said the Spirit of the Lord had consecrated him to proclaim "the recovery of sight to the blind." The world into which Jesus came was in a terrible state of moral darkness and spiritual blindness. No relief was in sight. These people who walked around in intense darkness despaired that light would ever come.

Jesus came into this darkened world as light. He quickly discovered that "people loved darkness rather than light because their deeds were evil" (John 3:19). In other cases people pulled down the blinds to shut out the light. This did not destroy the light, but left people in darkness nonetheless.

Until Jesus came as light, countless people lived in a world of darkness and blindness. They had good questions but no place to go for answers. It is not uncommon for people to go through periods of searching, doubting, questioning, experimentation, and confusion. Where are they to go for help?

Jesus would say that the church must be a place where good questions get good answers, where sincere doubt meets mature faith, and where confusion meets stability. Put a sign in front of the church that reads, "Ask your questions here." After all, he promised "Ask, and it will be given you; search, and you will find; knock, and the door will be opened for you" (Matt 7:7).

Fourth, is not the church a place where we can have a second chance? If not, where can I go to try again? Jesus said the Spirit of the Lord had instructed him "to set at liberty those who are oppressed." Many people have been bruised by their constant falling and failing. When one has sinned grievously, where is he or she to go for help? Many are broken victims of disappointment, failure, weakness, or embarrassment. They have tried and failed over and over again.

They say, "How can God still love me? He must be sick and tired of me by now. I have no right to come to him again. I have sinned away my day of grace. I may as well quit trying." They slip into worship, sit on the back row, try not to be noticed, say their hasty "God be merciful to me a sinner," and slip out again.

Is there a gospel of a second chance? Can John Mark, the deserter, ever be profitable to Paul in ministry again? Can vacillating Simon ever become Peter, the rock? Moses never crossed Jordan, his final finish line, but died without reaching the Promised Land. When Jesus died on the cross, God took the worst deed of history and turned it into the greatest victory—resurrection.

Can you hear Jesus saying, "We don't need another place for playing games, wearing masks, pretending to be something we are not, or trying to impress others that we are always on top of things." Rather, he would present the church as a place where those who have fallen can get up again. It is in the church that we hear failure is not final; there is always another chance.

People will seek out the church that is a fellowship of loving concern where our tears are understood and heart cries are heard, spirit can take wings, questions can be asked, and failures are not final. We make a great contribution to kingdom service when we contribute to the creation of such a church.

# Notes

[1]Ken Medema, "If This Is Not a Place," Waco TX: Word Music. Used by permission.

[2]This introduction is drawn from Lavonn D. Brown, *The Life of the Church* (Nashville: Broadman Press, 1987) 12-14.

[3]For the outline in this section see Dale Moody, "The Nature of the Church," in *What Is the Church?* Ed. Duke McCall (Nashville: Broadman Press, 1958) 15-27. See also Brown, 16-20.

# Free to Serve

## *William R. O'Brien*

I have heard of your faith in the Lord Jesus and your love toward all the saints, and for this reason I do not cease to give thanks for you as I remember you in my prayers. I pray that the God of our Lord Jesus Christ, the Father of glory, may give you a spirit of wisdom and revelation as you come to know him, so that, with the eyes of your heart enlightened, you may know what is the hope to which he has called you, what are the riches of his glorious inheritance among the saints, and what is the immeasurable greatness of his power for us who believe, according to the working of his great power. God put this power to work in Christ when he raised him from the dead and seated him at his right hand in the heavenly places, far above all rule and authority and power and dominion, and above every name that is named, not only in this age but also in the age to come. And he has put all things under his feet and has made him the head over all things for the church, which is his body, the fullness of him who fills all in all. (Eph 1:15-23)

There it was. I couldn't miss it. Even though I was careening around a curve on the outskirts of Gastonia, North Carolina, almost late to a speaking engagement nearby, I couldn't miss it. A small church building was positioned far back from the road. You could miss that. But you could not miss the big sign beside the road identifying the church. The name of the church was in the upper portion of the sign. You could miss that. But you could not miss the big block letters positioned in the middle of the sign: WORLD OUTREACH CENTER. Managing to keep the car on the road around the curve, I chuckled at the contrast between the size of the little building, and the self-perception of those who met inside. WORLD OUTREACH CENTER?

Then I sobered, engaging in a dialogue with myself: "They've got it. They understand what it means to be church. So what if they're not reaching every corner of the globe personally or congregationally, they've got the concept!" For the rest of the journey to speak at an annual Baptist association meeting, I wished out loud that such a sign could be erected outside every Baptist church building, flagging for the world that which is our top priority.

"Missions has been called the largest word in the Baptist vocabulary. No other ministry has done more to define who Baptists are and what we are about,"[1] says church historian, Leon McBeth. At least that may have been true the last 200 years. But throughout their 400-year history, the passion for freedom has been a dominant theme of Baptists, long before missions became a priority.

It is at this intersection, freedom and missions, that Baptists have an inherent problem. The freedom passion relates to the issue of autonomy. No bishop or hierarchy tells Baptists what to do or how to do it. The American culture reflected in rugged individualism and a macho mindset relates to the freedom issue in a subtle way. But, not to worry. The Bible comes to our rescue. We are people of the Book, and we believe what it says, right? In our "private" devotionals we read the various proof-texts of missions, such as "Go into all the world." Insidiously, however, privacy, piety, and freedom get intertwined in ways that run counter to the spirit of God's very mission.

A privatization of our faith and a polity of autonomy can be a deadening and deadly combination. It can justify isolation and insulation, rationalizing we must take care of our own first. Or, it can embolden a person and a single congregation to launch out in a world venture because "God told me to do it," and therefore there is no need to check with anyone or try to understand if God may be up to something in the larger body of Christ. What brings freedom and missions together? And what provides the restraint that yokes the sovereignty of God and the autonomy of the churches?

## A Covenant of Life

Baptist kinds of Christ-followers share much in common. Deep discussions can be held about our common beliefs, doctrines, and practices. But one distinct commonality is fellowship. When Baptists are at their best, they love to get together. The importance of Baptist World Alliance meetings far exceeds the content of programs. Baptist persons feel exhilarated in the discovery that there are many others out there "like us" who love Jesus and are trying to serve the kingdom. Especially is this true among small groups of Baptists in areas of religious or political oppression. It is easy to feel that one is all alone, or that no one else cares.

This reality came home to me vividly in our first month in Indonesia as newly-arrived missionaries. I traveled from Bandung, where we studied the language, to the capital city of Jakarta to handle some documents at the U.S. Embassy. When I emerged from the consul's office, a fine looking Indonesian man was standing in the foyer. Being young and gung-ho to meet all the Indonesians possible, I approached and introduced myself. The man spoke a little English in broken accent. He was able to communicate that he was an architect. His goal was to travel to the United States and study various architectural motifs in some of our cities.

By this time we had left the embassy building and were walking down one of Jakarta's main streets. Since I spoke little Indonesian at that point, and he spoke less English, we fell into silence as we walked together. Suddenly, he looked at me and said, "I Baptist." Surprised and excited, I responded in kind, "I'm Baptist." He threw his arms around my shoulders, and I his, as we walked arm-in-arm down this major thoroughfare. No United Nations charter, Indonesian-American Friendship Society, or any other human organization could have evoked the feeling of oneness that we two Baptist men felt at that moment.

Obviously, it was the "Christ in us" reality that made for oneness, more than a Baptist identity. But having said that, there was also a unique bond because of the Baptist way we expressed our commitment to the Christ and our discovery that God was working in a much larger arena than my own.

The kind of fellowship I refer to runs much deeper than get-togethers, snacks, or insulated holy huddles away from the cold, cruel world. I am talking about a fellowship that is the fruit of a covenant —a covenant that we neither initiated nor could keep alive on our own, a covenant of grace and truth initiated by the God of grace and truth, a grace that loves us in our sin, and a truth that sets us free. But graced and set free for what? The answer to that question is what the Bible is all about.

The Creator-Redeemer God made a covenant with Abraham that, through him, all the racial and ethnic groups of the world would be blessed (Gen 12:1-3). In his vision on the isle of Patmos, John saw persons of every race, tribe, and tongue around the throne giving praise to the Lamb who is worthy (Rev 7:9). Sacred Scripture reveals both the purpose and plan of the ages whereby all God's purposes will be brought to completion. Between Genesis and Revelation lies the unfolding saga of the first covenant people and the continuing story through the expanded covenant people, known as the church. The church has no mission of its own. It lives as both sign and agent of the kingdom of God, and is servant to the mission of God.

The fellowship of the church characterizes a colony of heaven planted within the unbelieving world. One of the main priorities of the church is to guard zealously the fellowship. A healthy and harmonious kind of church must always be alert so that nothing mars the cutting-edge witness of the covenant body. It is that qualitative difference between the church and the world that draws others into its life like a magnet. That is the centripetal force of the church. Then, dispersed like salt and light into the marketplaces, members of the body of Christ live out the same quality of life that is both confounding and contagious. That is the centrifugal force of the church.

Again, when Baptists are at their best, they love to get together. And when they do, others long to experience that kind of life. The apostle Paul reminded believers and churches in the area of modern-day Turkey,

> But now in Christ Jesus you who were once far off have been brought near by the blood of Christ. For, he is our peace; in his flesh he has made both groups into one and has broken down the dividing wall, that is, the hostility between us. . . . So then you are no longer strangers and aliens, but you are citizens with the saints and also members of the household of God, built upon the foundation of the apostles and prophets, with Christ Jesus himself as the cornerstone. In him the whole structure is joined together and grows into a holy temple in the Lord; in whom you also are built together spiritually into a dwelling place for God. (Eph 2:13-14, 19-22)

# A Covenant of Hope

Most of the Baptists I have been around are very active people. In fact, someone half-jokingly said the reason she did not join a Baptist church was that she didn't have the energy and strength to be a member. We have programs running out our ears. Many of them are good and needed. When Baptists are at their best, they give of themselves in unselfish service, locally and globally. Why? Because they understand that the covenant agreement yokes us together with God in a comanagerial role of God's mission.

It is at this crucial intersection, covenant and culture, that Baptists have an inherent problem. Not only does the American culture accommodate itself within an autonomous and privatized mindset; it seems to reward a go-it-alone mentality. Mix in a penchant for numbers with a competitive spirit, and there emerges an ecclesial metabolism that produces programmatic hyperactivity. Who says Baptists are not a liturgical people? Our most sacred liturgy is getting in one room and counting each other. If there were some cataclysmic event that destroyed every person on earth but three Baptists, they would immediately meet, organize, elect a president, vice-president, secretary-treasurer, and set an impossible goal of four for the next Sunday!

Another deadly combination is that of being goal-driven mixed with the art of entertainment. "Market sensitivity" may match up with the spiritual urge to meet people at the point of their needs. But how easy it is to step across a fine line, doing whatever it takes to "get them in the door." It would be tragic if the broad way that leads to destruction led people through the front door of an entertainment center masquerading as a church.

But there is another kind of hope revealed in Scripture. Again, in Paul's letter to believers in the area of Ephesus he told them how he was praying for them:

> I pray that the God of our Lord Jesus Christ, the Father of glory, may give you a spirit of wisdom and revelation as you come to know him, so that, with the eyes of your heart enlightened, you may know what is the hope to which he has called you. (Eph 1:17-18a)

What is the hope to which we are called? Professor William Owen Carver taught at Southern Baptist Theological Seminary for about forty years. He was a visionary in the field of world missions. He was also a noted Greek scholar. Carver spent his life plumbing the depths of the Ephesian letter. His knowledge of Greek in general, and the thrust of Paul's application in this Ephesian letter in particular, led him to translate Ephesians 1:18 with a twist that undergirds the entire theme of the letter:

> making definite mention of you in my praying . . . so that you may know by insight what is (God's) hope (in the people and plan) of his calling.[2]

The covenant-making God placed great hope in those being called alongside to be stewards of the mystery of God. Believers are called in to be comanagers of the open secret of God's love for all creation. Can you imagine such a thing?

Once overtaken by such an overwhelming thought, I have been saddened to admit how often I personally and our churches collectively have frustrated the very hope God placed in us. Such hope postponed is not the result of a lack of the presence or power of God to accomplish the purposes of God. Paul clearly indicates "what is the immeasurable greatness of his power for us who believe, according to the working of his great power" (Eph 1:19). One of the commissions Christ left for his followers, and the church through all ages, surrounds the imperative to disciple the ethnic peoples of the world with the assurance of his own authority/power and the promise of his presence (Matt 28:18-20).

Since God knows our finiteness and weakness, why place hope in the likes of us? Perhaps the only one who is worthy of praise and honor gets even greater glory when enabling hope to be fulfilled as it is channeled through weak, clay pots such as us. When Baptists are at their best, they are not planning programs. Rather, they are at their best when they are in the process of becoming all they possibly can in Christ Jesus. In so doing they make themselves available to the God of mission to be used anywhere, in any way. Have you ever wondered if God may giggle just a bit in the joy of seeing children of God fulfilling the purpose for which they were made?

## Conclusion

Life and hope. Free and faithful. Baptists are committed to those realized ideals. We have done our share of serious arguing and fighting across the years because we do hold such things in high regard. But too often open dialogue disintegrates. Our energies are consumed in staging events and extravaganzas to hype our programs. We convene and pass resolutions on issues that burn a hole in our emotions. But when Baptists are at their best, they don't get their identity or motivation for service from events.

Longtime friend Bruce McIver shared with me a quotation by Willie Morris from *A Southern Album*. Willie Morris pays deep respect to his heritage rooted in Mississippi and writes of the endurance of the South:

> It endured because of its human beings: its black people, its white people, its politicians, its characters, its writers. For history is not events, . . . it is people acting and living their past in the present.[3]

McIver picks up on that to muse,

> Perhaps that is what the Christian faith is all about. Unfortunately, we measure everything by "events"—what happened, to whom, when, how? Thus, we "document" life . . . event by event. I'm struggling here, but

the Church, the Kingdom, the Fellowship, the Mission does not consist merely of events . . . conventions . . . decrees . . . resolutions . . . bad events . . . good events. . . . It is the "people of faith" . . . diverse . . . different . . . black and white . . . living the past in the present.[4]

And I would add that the covenant of hope means we are proactively living the future in the present.

When Baptists are at their best, they are free to serve. They look at the past. Around the Communion table they remember that a covenant-making God has brought them thus far. They turn to the future as God's hope for the faithless and the hopeless. And therefore,

> to him who by the power at work within us is able to accomplish abundantly far more than all we can ask or imagine, to him be glory in the church and Christ Jesus to all generations, forever and ever. Amen. (Eph 3:20-21)

# Notes

[1]Leon McBeth, "The Legacy of the Baptist Missionary Society," *Baptist History and Heritage* 37/3 (July 1992): 3.

[2]W. O. Carver, *The Glory of God in the Christian Calling* (Nashville: Broadman Press, 1949; paperback edition, 1979) 192.

[3]Cited in Irvin Glusker, ed., *A Southern Album* (Birmingham AL: Oxmoor House, 1976) 9.

[4]Personal conversation.

# The Church Christ Builds

## Daniel Vestal

Now when Jesus came into the district of Caesarea Philippi, he asked his disciples, "Who do people say that Son of Man is?" And they said, "Some say John the Baptist, but others Elijah, and still others Jeremiah or one of the prophets." He said to them, "But who do you way that I am?" Simon Peter answered, "You are the Messiah, the Son of the living God." And Jesus answered him, "Blessed are you, Simon son of Jonah! For flesh and blood has not revealed this to you, but my Father in heaven. And I tell you, you are Peter, and on this rock I will build my church, and the gates of Hades will not prevail against it. I will give you the keys of the kingdom of heaven, and whatever you bind on earth will be bound in heaven, and whatever you loose on earth will be loosed in heaven." Then he sternly ordered the disciples not to tell anyone that he was the Messiah.

From that time on, Jesus began to show his disciples that he must go to Jerusalem and undergo great suffering at the hands of the elders and chief priests and scribes, and be killed, and on the third day be raised. And Peter took him aside and began to rebuke him, saying, "God forbid it, Lord! This must never happen to you." But he turned and said to Peter, "Get behind me, Satan! You are a stumbling block to me; for you are setting your mind not on divine things but on human things."

Then Jesus told his disciples, "If any want to become my followers, let them deny themselves and take up their cross and follow me." (Matt 16:13-24)

The church of Jesus Christ is a grand and glorious fellowship. We use many words to describe it, but they are all limiting, because the church is greater than all descriptive adjectives. We speak of the church as being apostolic, catholic, reformed, evangelical, free, charismatic. But all of these adjectives cannot exhaust the fullness of its meaning.

## A Universal Fellowship

The church transcends time, space, geography, and theological differences. I believe it is important to see the church from this perspective and see it in the broadest and most inclusive dimension. When God in divine glory sees the church, God sees it as a whole. And when Christ said, "I will build my church," he was speaking of a realty that knows no division. God's great plan of redemption is to rescue from sinful humanity "a chosen generation, a royal priesthood, a holy nation, God's own people" (1 Pet 2:9).

When in glory the church of Jesus Christ is presented as a bride, beautifully dressed, it will not be Baptist or Methodist or nondenominational. It will not be American, African, or Chinese. It will not be first, tenth, or twentieth century. It will be the church through the ages across theological spectrum from every tribe, tongue, and nation. Though it is invisible to us, it is not invisible to God. We ought to live as though we believe in this universal fellowship and act toward others who believe in Christ as though we belong to each other.

Of course, we have differences; but we respect each other, trust each other, and treat each other with love because we believe we are the body of Christ across our differences. One of the secrets of renewal in our day is for us to see a grand vision of the church, to have a high view of the church, and then out of that vision to live, pray, and work. Of course, what is visible to us today is a fragmented, fractured church. But what is visible to God is one church. And what will be presented to Christ is a purified, glorified, and triumphal church. It will include the redeemed from all time and ages.

## Local Fellowship

The church that Christ builds is not only a universal fellowship; it is a local fellowship. The New Testament word for church, *ekklesia*, literally means "the called-out ones." It is an assembly or group of believers that gather in one place and one time. Eighty percent of the time in the New Testament when the word church is used, it defines a local, particular congregation.

The church Christ builds is not exclusively in the universal dimension, but also in the local, congregational dimension. You can't have one without the other. The person who says, "I love the church of Jesus Christ, worldwide and universal, but I don't love any one local church," is speaking a contradiction. And the opposite is true. One who says, "I love one specific church, but I don't love the church universal" is also speaking contradiction.

I believe when Christ promised to build his church, he was speaking of the church both in its universal and local dimensions. These words are a great encouragement to me as a pastor, because Christ himself is the builder. We work and labor, but in the final analysis, only Christ can save a soul, renew a spirit, change a life, form a body of believers. He is the builder. A church is not like other organizations, institutions, or corporations. It is divinely ordained and constructed. This means that since Christ builds his church, it is his church and not ours. We affectionately speak of a church as my church or our church, but it's not. It's Christ's church.

## How Christ Builds His Church

Christ builds his church with people. What kind of people? With people like Peter. Christ uses *flawed people* to build his church. Jesus said, "I have come to call not the righteous but sinners to repentance" (Luke 5:32). Christ builds his church with sinners. It was true of the first disciples, and it is true today. Those first disciples were anything but a well-mannered, well-groomed, and well-respected bunch. They were a most unlikely nucleus. Peter was an obnoxious, and at times, profane man. James and John were hotheaded, so much so that Jesus called them "sons of thunder." Many of the women who associated with Jesus were known for their sexual immorality and demon possession. Yet these are the ones Jesus called to follow him. They surely didn't "have it all together"—morally, spiritually, or socially. They were flawed.

So are we. To say that you and I are flawed is not to say we are worthless. Sin is not worthlessness. I can remember when we used to sing the old gospel song,

> Alas, and did my Savior bleed
> And did my Sovereign die
> Would he devote that sacred head
> For such a worm as I.

I'm glad the editors of our hymnal changed the text, because I never did see myself as a worm. People have taken verses that attribute sinfulness to human personality and used them to attribute worthlessness to human personality. To see myself as a sinner, does not mean I see myself as worthless.

Also to see myself as a sinner doesn't mean I see myself as a victim. There are some who know they have messed up their lives and done bad things, but they refuse to accept responsibility for it. They think that they are sinners because of ignorance, circumstances, or environment. They say something like this: "I know I am a sinner, but really I couldn't help myself. Look at my parents. I was born in the wrong time. I didn't know any better. I had a bad childhood. I have a bad marriage. I have a learning disability."

I realize that people are victimized by ignorance and poverty, and that we need to do all we can to address those problems, but every person is more than a victim. Every person is a responsible human being who can make choices. I saw a cartoon of a young delinquent who had admitted to the judge of committing a crime. His defense attorney said, "Judge, please pardon this young man. Given his heredity and environment, he didn't have a choice." But the biblical message is that he did have a choice. All have choices.

This begins to get to the very meaning of sin, and this begins to get at the heart of what it means to see myself as flawed. To see myself as a sinner means to see myself as a responsible person who has made bad choices against God. I have done it intentionally. I didn't do it accidentally or casually, but deliberately and consciously.

My bad choices are not just mistakes. I am not just frail, limited, and weak. If we think of human sinfulness only in terms of human frailty, human limitation, or human weakness, we have not plumbed the depth of human sinfulness. It is possible to make bad choices that are mistakes because we don't know any better. But sin is a bad choice even when we do know better. To see myself as flawed means I accept full responsibility for my sin, I am genuinely sorry for it, and I desire to change.

The church is a community of sinners. It is a community of people who see ourselves and each other as sinners. We are not an exclusive club made up of the elite or those who have it all together. We don't have to perform for each other or impress each other with how good we are. Our expectations of each other do not demand perfection, and we're not surprised at our stumbling. We're transparent with each other, confessing our faults to one another, praying for one another, and bearing one another's burdens. Christ builds his church with flawed people.

Christ also builds his church with *favored people*, or graced people. That is another way of saying that he builds with those who have discovered the love and grace of God. That's what happened to Simon Peter at Caesarea Philippi. After he confessed Jesus as Messiah, he was told, "Flesh and blood has not revealed this to you, but my Father in Heaven" (Matt 16:17). Flawed as he was, Simon Peter discovered grace. He experienced grace. With such people Christ builds his church. Those individuals who not only know themselves to be fallen, but know an even greater reality, become the church. That reality is the love and grace of God.

Love is the essential character of God. Because God is God, God is holy. God is other than we are. All the words we use to describe God speak of this otherness, transcendence, omnipresence, omniscience, omnipotence. God is the eternal Thou, the never created, always existent ultimate reality. Or to use the biblical word, God is spirit. But the incredible and wonderful news is that this Holy One, this eternal and divine presence, is in God's very essence, personal, outgoing benevolence, essential goodness. God is love, and everything that God does proceeds from that love. God creates out of love. God creates for love. God relates to us in love. All the universe is a revelation of the love of God. Everything God does, God does from love because of love. God's love for us is unconditional. God is the divine lover, and we are the beloved.

Because God's essential character is love, God acts toward us in grace. And grace proceeds from God's goodness. God shows goodness by divine grace. If love is the word that describes how God is in God's self, and how this divine relationship is to us in creation, then grace is the word that describes how God relates to us in our need. Grace is God's disposition and provision for us in our condition, in our fallenness, our fracturedness, our flawedness. Grace is God's disposition toward us while we are sinners. Grace is God's solution for our unresolved problem. Grace is God's cure for our incurable disease. Grace is God's remedy for our healing. I like to define God's grace as God in love providing what we need but do not deserve.

To discover grace means conversion and radical change. Conversion means that I realize the answer to my flawedness is not works; that is, try harder, do more, be good, act nice, and then God will help you. Conversion means that I realize the answer to my flawedness is not law; that is, obey the rules, conform to the standard, keep the commandments, and then things will get better. Conversion means that I realize the answer to my flawedness is not performance; that is, look good, go to church, wear nice clothes, have good manners, and everything will turn out okay. Conversion means that I realize the answer to my flawedness is not manipulation and negotiation: that is, let's make a deal; if you'll do this, then God you do that,;or thinking that God helps those who helps themselves. Conversion means I realize that the only answer to my sinfulness and brokenness is grace. Christ builds his church with people who have discovered grace.

We are able to see and say, "You are the Christ, the Son of the living God." This is what Scripture calls faith. When Jesus said to Simon, "Upon this rock I will build my church," he was saying, "I will build my church with *people of faith*." Jesus was saying to Simon, "I will build my church with people who know themselves to be flawed but have discovered grace and then accepted it."

The hard facts are that it is possible to reject the grace of God. Some receive grace and live by faith; others reject grace and live without it. Some are dependent on grace; others insist on being self-dependent. Some are saved; some are lost. Some recognize their sin and need and trust Christ; others refuse. God offers us grace, but God doesn't force us to receive it.

But once we receive it, we become like Peter. We join a blessed company of the believing. We become part of a real family—a family of faith. Who are the ones Christ uses to build his church? It is not necessarily the most beautiful, the most gifted, the most powerful, the most successful. In fact, at times it is the exact opposite. But it is those who by faith have received grace and made their confession of Jesus as God's Son.

## Conclusion

Recently on a Sunday night after church, my wife and I went to a restaurant. In the course of the evening I heard a boy swearing and shouting at his father. As I looked, I could tell that the teenage boy was mentally retarded and for some reason was very angry. He continued his tirade, but the father gently stood there receiving his abuse. Finally, both left the restaurant together.

After we finished our meal, my wife and I walked past this father and son still standing outside in conversation. By now the son was subdued and obviously ashamed. But still the father in his gentle way was listening and talking. As I drove off the parking lot, I saw one of the tenderest scenes of my life. I watched as that father put his arms around his son and drew him to himself.

The contrite son bowed his head on his father's shoulder and then put his arms around his father's waist. They both stood there in an embrace for an extended period of time. I was so touched that I stopped my car and watched with tears in my eyes. Finally, they both walked to their car, arm in arm.

I thought to myself, that's what God has done to and for us. In our anger we have shouted at God, sinned against God, abused God. Yet in divine love and grace, God has reached out to us and embraced us. God has provided for our needs in Jesus Christ and awakened faith in our hearts. Our feeble faith is not much more than that boy putting his arms around his father's waist. Yet God knows that. God honors that, blesses that, and uses that. Our confession and commitment are but responses to grace. Beyond that we walk arm in arm. Jesus actually partners with us and uses us to build his church, both universal and local. We actually become a part of what God is doing in the world. What a grand and glorious privilege to be a part of the church of the Lord Jesus Christ!

# The Servant People of God

## Brad Creed

> James and John, the sons of Zebedee, came forward to him and said to him, "Teacher, we want you to do for us whatever we ask of you." And he said to them, "What is it you want me to do for you?" And they said to him, "Grant us to sit, one at your right hand and one at your left, in your glory," But Jesus said to them, "You do not know what you are asking. Are you able to drink the cup that I drink, or be baptized with the baptism that I am baptized with?" They replied, "We are able." Then Jesus said to them, "The cup that I drink you will drink; and with the baptism with which I am baptized, you will be baptized; but to sit at my right hand or at my left is not mine to grant, but it is for those for whom it has been prepared."
>
> When the ten heard this, they began to be angry with James and John. So Jesus called them and said to them, "You know that among the Gentiles those whom they recognize as their rulers lord it over them, and their great ones are tyrants over them. But it is not so among you; but whoever wishes to become great among you must be your servant, and whoever wishes to be first among you must be slave of all. For the Son of Man came not to be served but to serve, and to give his life a ransom for many." (Mark 10:35-45)

Baptist Christians gather together as the church based upon their common confession of faith in Christ. They are "discontinuity people," called out from their own worlds within the larger world to be the people of God. The new life that they share together in Christ, which is a gift from God, is powerfully symbolized by the ordinance of baptism. Whenever two or three or four or four hundred gather together in their common confession of the lordship of Christ, which is imaged through the practice of baptism, there is the beginning of a believers' church.

But where two or three Baptists gather together as the church, there are usually at least four or five opinions. Beyond the common confession and the rite of baptism, Baptists share life together in a community with its rich diversity.

# The Church: A Life of Service

If the believers' church is constituted by a common confession of faith, it finds its continuation and integrity in the life of service. Servanthood enables believers to live into and up to their common confession of faith. The believing people of God are also the servant people of God.

Albert Schweitzer, one of the most gifted men of this century, gained notoriety for his accomplishments as a New Testament scholar, learned theologian, skilled physician, and accomplished musician. The world will forever remember him, however, as a selfless servant who left behind the security of his accomplishments in Europe to be a missionary doctor in Africa. Regarding his own great aspiration in life, Schweitzer said: "One thing I know: the only ones among you who will be really happy are those who will have sought and found how to serve."[1]

Jesus himself stated that his aspiration in life was "not to be served, but to serve, and give his life a ransom for many" (Mark 10:45). He calls the church to serve in his spirit, and the standard that he elevates in pursuing this mission is "whoever wishes to become great among you must be your servant" (Mark 10:43).

Some of Jesus' followers wanted to be great but didn't understand that greatness in the kingdom of God is tied to servanthood. Two of those disciples, James and John, found it difficult to make a distinction between the kind of greatness that is the fruit of servanthood and the kind of greatness that is fueled by an unguarded ambition. These two brothers, descriptively nicknamed the "Sons of Thunder," came to Jesus with a brash request: "Teacher, we want you to do for us whatever we ask of you" (Mark 10:35). Jesus indulged them momentarily by responding, "What is it you want me to do for you?" (Mark 10:36). They answered: "Grant us to sit, one on your right hand and one at your left, in your glory" (Mark 10:37). They treated Jesus as a means to an end, like a credit card with no borrowing limit. What was the nature of their overweening ambition that they would make such a brazen claim upon Christ?

The location of this text in the Gospel of Mark is important for understanding the dynamics of the dialogue between Jesus and the sons of Zebedee. This passage comes right after Jesus' teaching on the rich young ruler (Mark 10:17-31) and the sobering announcement of his impending death in Jerusalem (Mark 10:32-34). Did they rationalize that, in spite of Jesus' warning about the rich young ruler, they were different or somehow deserving of the more desirable places in Jesus' coming kingdom? Or did they sense in Jesus' prediction of his own passion that his ministry was drawing to a fateful and disappointing conclusion, so that it was now or never if they were to have a shot at greatness? After all, fortune smiles on the aggressive, and if nothing is ventured, nothing is gained.

It is uncertain what motivated their brash request, but ironically and even tragically, after all they had seen Jesus do and say regarding the nature of his kingdom and the direction of his own ministry, they simply did not get it. They desired Jesus' power but failed to see that the means for appropriating his power was not through grasping but by yielding. Their ambition was for personal standing, yet Jesus taught that true greatness is reflected in servanthood.

This passage is a reminder to the church, the servant people of God, that the church is to be different from the world. Jesus warned his followers about the secular rulers of his time who exercised a harsh authority over their subjects (Mark 10:42). The church, because of its Lord, whose presence it extends into the world, is not to model a communal life comparable to secular power structures. Jesus reminded his disciples that worldly leadership is domineering and authoritarian. In so warning them, he did not attempt to correct worldly leadership. He merely stated what should be obvious to those who follow him in the way of the cross and consequently challenged his people to reject secular leadership models that empower hierarchies at the expense of the servant gifts of all the people of God. Regardless of what the church might learn from current concepts of leadership and organizational structure, it dares not neglect the gifts of its own resources that are derived from its character and calling as the servant people of God.

The consequences of grasping for position and power undermine the integrity of the church and ultimately its ability to extend to others the ministry of Jesus. Such an effect became readily apparent to Jesus' other ten disciples who, when they heard the request from the sons of Zebedee, became indignant (Mark 10:41). This kind of ambition in the body is divisive. It fractures community because the focus turns to the standing or position of each member rather than to the collective commitment to and practice of servanthood.

What would have happened had Jesus granted the audacious request of James and John? There still would have been the matter to resolve of who would sit at the right side of Jesus and who would sit at the left. In biblical imagery, the right side is the preferred side. The right side of the throne is the most honorable position to occupy. The right hand of God is the most powerful hand. In fact, it is doubtful, according to biblical allusions, whether God even has a left hand. Had Jesus said, "Granted as you wish! One of you brothers may sit at my right and the other at my left," there would have been a conflagration of sibling rivalry. The other ten disciples acted as though they were sufficiently incensed by the naked opportunism of the Zebedee boys. Truth be told, however, it was probably not the spiritual blindness of James and John that offended them. They were indignant because these two launched a pre-preemptive strike that jeopardized their own ambitions for glory.

## The Jesus Way

Jesus played referee before he assumed the role of teacher, and once he diffused the hostilities, he called the disciples to him so that he could teach them about *his* way to greatness. His way to greatness is serving in the spirit of humility. Humility is never easy to understand or practice, especially in an age when people are preoccupied with their own advancement and organizations are concerned about their own survival. Common images of humility degenerate into stereotypes, such as the doormat upon which are wiped the feet of the rich and powerful or the servile groveling of an inferior in the presence of a superior. This, of course, is not the style of humility Jesus commends to his servant people.

A helpful way to understand the essential quality of humility is to consider words that are similar in derivation or spelling. One word is *humus*, which is the rich loam of organic existence that makes growth and fertility possible. Humility, in the experience of the people of God, should be down-to-earth so that the church is connected to the nitty-gritty of life. The other word that is similar is *humor*, which certainly would add the welcomed factor of levity and even grace to the experience of humility. G. K. Chesterton reminded us that "angels can fly because they take themselves lightly."[2]

In the teachable moment that followed, Jesus revealed that nothing for the Kingdom could be gained by grasping or seeking advantage over others. Not only did Jesus teach this, but this kind of humility describes the movement of his life and ministry. The downward mobility of Jesus is lyrically celebrated in a passage in the book of Philippians that announces that although Christ

> was in the form of God, [he] did not regard equality with God as something to be exploited, but emptied himself, taking the form of a slave, being born in human likeness. And being found in human form, he humbled himself and became obedient to the point of death—even death on a cross. Therefore God also highly exalted him and gave him the name that is above every name, so that at the name of Jesus every knee should bend, in heaven and on earth and under the earth, and every tongue should confess that Jesus Christ is Lord, to the glory of God the Father. (2:5-11)

## The Church: Imitating the Jesus Way

Like its Lord, the church puts itself in a position to serve others by humbling itself in obedience to God. The nature of Jesus and the nature of his body, the church, are not characterized by selfish grabbing but by selfless giving. The exaltation of Christ that this passage describes and the eventual glorification that the church will experience is not a reward but a consequence of this humility. The position that James and John sought can be realized only by the way of humiliation.

Like their Lord, the servant people of God get involved and identify with humanity. On one occasion in the ministry of Jesus, religious leaders dragged before him a woman who had been accused of adultery. In bringing her before Jesus, they were motivated as much by the desire to entrap Jesus as they were to condemn the woman. While they hurled their accusations at her and posed their moral challenges to Jesus, he did something rather unusual. He knelt on the ground and began writing in the dirt. What he was writing, if anything, is unknown, but this activity symbolically portrayed his willingness to come down to her level, in the grime of her own shame, and to get involved with her. In so doing, Jesus showed the church what true greatness is (John 7:53–8:11).

Another time Jesus gathered with his disciples for a meal. While they made the necessary preparations, he girded himself with a towel, poured water into a basin, and began to wash the feet of his disciples. They were shocked at his actions because this was considered menial work normally consigned to the servants. The disciples protested, but Jesus insisted that he do this because his way is servanthood. He showed the church what true greatness is by getting involved (John 13:1-17).

Often the church's desire to serve is like the woman who enrolled in a first aid class because she wanted to help people. She successfully completed the course and received her certificate of accomplishment. One of her friends asked her if she had been able to put her training to use. "Oh yes," she replied. "Just last week when I was driving home from work, I came upon a terrible automobile accident with major injuries. I was so proud of myself. I knew exactly what to do. I sat down on the curb, put my head between my knees, and did not even begin to faint."

The servant people of God roll up their sleeves and use their training in humility to get involved with people in their difficulties. They bind wounds, wipe away tears, and embrace the unlovable. If the church desires greatness, it pursues greatness by the route of servanthood. Sometimes Jesus leads his church to people who are lost, hurting, confused, and otherwise difficult to deal with. Servanthood compels the church to identify with people as Jesus did.

The servant people of God also understand that it does not take much to make a difference for the kingdom of God. Jesus chose only twelve men into whom to pour his life. On this occasion highlighted in the Gospel of Mark, even these twelve had trouble understanding what Jesus was about. He nevertheless made the effort and took the risk of entrusting them with the ministry of the kingdom, knowing that it doesn't take much to make a difference. When Jesus described the nature of faith, he did not compare it to mountains or boulders but to a mustard seed that, though minuscule, will yield something of significance when it gives of itself and dies (Matt 13:31-31).

Jesus compared a true servant to the good shepherd. This shepherd is called good because he is willing to leave ninety-nine sheep safely in the fold for just one who has strayed and is lost (Matt 18:10-14). It does not take much to make a difference in the kingdom.

Early one morning as a man walked along the beach, he noticed a beachcomber in the distance. While the surf rolled in on the shore, he watched the beachcomber picking up something and throwing it back into the ocean. Over and over he did this. The man came closer and saw that the beachcomber was picking up starfish that were washed in by the tide. As the waves rolled in more starfish, one by one he picked them up and threw them back into the ocean. As far as one could look down the edge of the shoreline, there were starfish stranded by the action of the waves. When the man came within speaking distance of the beachcomber, he asked him what he was doing. Acting somewhat perturbed because he had been momentarily distracted from his important activity, the beachcomber replied, "Can't you see what I'm doing. I'm saving these starfish." The man said, "There must be hundreds and hundreds of starfish along this beach. You can't make a difference by what you are doing." The beachcomber replied as he held up yet another stranded starfish, "It makes a difference to this one," and he threw it into the ocean and resumed his activity.[3]

The servant people of God understand that, through faithfulness to Christ, it does not take much to make a difference for the kingdom. They serve their Lord one challenge, one opportunity, one person at a time.

The servant people of God also remember whom they serve. Christ calls his people to serve others because they are called first to serve him. Jesus himself insisted that his earthly mission was service. The church serves others because of its prior service to Christ. If the church is simply about the business of doing good and helping people in need, yet fails to see that it serves others precisely because it serves Christ, then it has become nothing more than a social-service agency or benevolent organization. When the church advances its position or agenda in the world without the governance of the universal Christ and the way of life he has established for the church, then the church is left only with its own preferences in a marketplace of competing options. When the church sets lofty goals and pursues missional objectives and casts noble visions and yet loses connection with the life-giving power of Christ whom the church serves, the result is frustration, burnout, and the barrenness of busyness.

We made a significant archaeological discovery in one of the churches that I served as pastor. Some of the official church records thought to have been lost turned up in a church member's attic. Church minutes and records are interesting to read because of what they say and sometimes because of what they don't say. In these records that had come to light, there were accounts of souls saved and sacrifices made. There were stories of courage and commitment as well as occasional revelations of strife and pettiness. Thumbing through the yellowed pages of the old book of minutes was, for me, a window into the glorious particularity of a Baptist congregation. I have since forgotten many of the details of that document except one. It was an entry that was dated around the turn of the twentieth century:

5:30 P. M. Thursday, May 16, 1901. Ladies Missionary Society met at the
church. Member present: Ida L. Stephens. Sang—*All the Way My Savior
Leads Me* and *Come Unto Me and Rest*. Read James second chapter.
Meeting adjourned. Signed, *Ida L. Stephens.*

Was this woman who recorded the minutes, in addition to being
the only member present, attempting to make her point to posterity
by reminding the other members of the society that she alone, like Elijah the prophet of old who reminded the Lord that he alone had not
bowed his knee to Baal (1 Kings 19:14), had been faithful while the
others were negligent in their duties? A more gracious revisionism
would prefer to believe that this was a woman who could show up
all by herself, read Scripture, and sing praise to God because she re-
membered whom she served. She understood that ultimately there is
only one audience that counts for the church. Her songs, her reading,
and even her attendance were acts of service to the one who did not
come to be served but to serve and thereby show his people their way
into the world.

# Notes

[1]Albert Schweitzer, cited in *Barnes and Noble Book of Quotations,* ed. Robert I.
Fitzhenry (New York: Barnes and Noble, 1981) 127.

[2]G. K. Chesterton, *Orthodoxy: The Romance of Faith* (New York: Doubleday,
1959) 120.

[3]Adapted from an essay by Loren Eisley, *The Star Thrower* (New York: Times
Books, 1978) 135-36.

# How Baptists Do Church

## *Howard W. Roberts*

I therefore, the prisoner in the Lord, beg you to lead a life worthy of the calling to which you have been called, with all humility and gentleness, with patience, bearing with one another in love, making every effort to maintain the unity of the Spirit in the bond of peace. There is one body and one Spirit, just as you were called to the one hope of your calling, one Lord, one faith, one baptism, one God and Father of all, who is above all the through all and in all.

But each of us was given grace according to the measure of Christ's gift. Therefore it is said, "when he ascended on high he made captivity itself a captive; he gave gifts to his people." (When it says, "He ascended," what does it mean but that he had also descended into the lower parts of the earth? He who descended is the same one who ascended far above all the heavens, so that he might fill all things.) The gifts he gave were that some would be apostles, some prophets, some evangelists, some pastors and teachers, to equip the saints for the work of ministry, for building up the body of Christ, until all of us come to the unity of the faith and of the knowledge of the Son of God, to maturity, to the measure of the full stature of Christ. We must no longer be children, tossed to and fro and blown about by every wind of doctrine, by people's trickery, by their craftiness in deceitful scheming. But speaking the truth in love, we must grow up in every way into him who is the head, into Christ, from whom the whole body, joined and knit together by every ligament with which it is equipped, as each part is working properly, promotes the body's growth in building itself up in love. (Eph 4:1-16)

How Baptists do church cannot be described in a vacuum. Other important issues, namely religious liberty and the priesthood of all believers, impact the way Baptists do church. Although the principles of religious liberty and the priesthood of believers are not the thrust of this sermon, they nourished the soil in which Baptist churches took root and grew.

Liberty and Freedom! Liberty and freedom defined and characterized Baptists from our beginnings in the 1600s. Two groups in England, the Puritans and the Separatists, grew out of the interests and emphases of Martin Luther and other reformers who saw the need for reform in the church. When leaders of the Church of England resisted such suggestions and dealt harshly with those who called for reforms, the desire and need for freedom became more intense. The Puritans wanted to *purify* the Church of England, while staying in the church. The Separatists, however, concluded that the only way to improve the church was to *separate* from the Church of England. Both of these groups greatly influenced people who became known by the derogatory term, "Anabaptists," the rebaptizers. Later, the term "Anabaptist" was shortened to Baptists. Like many religious groups, we Baptists are known by a name we did not choose for ourselves.

No doubt the greatest contribution Baptists have made to the landscape of religion has been the emphasis on religious liberty. When religious liberty is an essential part of the way people view life and express their faith, the priesthood of believers and the autonomy of the local congregation naturally follow. These three principles—religious liberty, the priesthood of believers, and the autonomy of the local congregation—are defining characteristics of Baptists. These characteristics have shaped the way Baptists have done church for over three hundred years. To the extent these characteristics are clearly practiced, people are authentic Baptists. To the extent these characteristics are distorted or ignored, people are not genuine Baptists.

As we turn our attention to how Baptists do church, some brief exploration of the priesthood of believers is necessary. In Baptist life this principle is at work on every level from the individual to the denominational, from local congregation to international organizations. Without an understanding of the priesthood of believers, we cannot understand how and why Baptists do church the way we do.

## Believers' Priesthood

The concept of every Christian being a priest, a minister, a servant in the name and cause of Christ is reflected throughout the Gospels and the letters of the New Testament. The Gospels clearly portray every disciple of Christ as a minister. This principle was evident in Jesus' ministry. He called disciples to learn from him and to be ministers with him. One hundred and twenty disciples joined with him, and while Jesus worked closely with twelve of them, a hierarchy of leadership never existed. Always the emphasis was on being servants, not leaders of power.

Not only in the Gospels, but throughout the letters of Paul, the priesthood of believers is an important concept. In writing to the churches at Corinth and Rome, Paul encouraged Christians to develop their gifts, abilities, and callings (1 Cor 12–14; Rom 12:3-8). A hierarchy of gifts never appears in Paul's lists. His lists of gifts are not exhaustive, only illustrative.

A clear similarity exists between Jesus' calling, his instructions to his disciples, and Paul's admonitions to members of the various churches. The priesthood of believers is never so individualistic as to suggest that believers are to be lone rangers. Quite the contrary, the emphasis is that believers are priests to each other and together to the world at large. Together, with their varied, unique, and individual gifts, these believer-priests form the body of Christ. Like the human body, each part has its function, but each must be a part of the whole. So it is with followers of Christ. Every Christian is a "part" of the larger body of Christ.

With the passing of time in Christian history, a more formal structure of leadership developed in the church. As a result, the division of labor became designated as "laity" and "clergy." Clergy often were the better educated people in a community. The gap between clergy and laity became wider and wider. Unfortunately and unbiblically, a class system evolved in the church.

In the fourth century, one of the worst things to happen to the early church occurred under Constantine. Constantine, the emperor of the Roman empire, became a Christian and ordered all of his soldiers baptized. What was good enough for the leader was good enough for the soldiers! The leader imposed his beliefs on his followers. Folklore says that Constantine had everything but the tips of their swords baptized. Some have suggested that this is when the church moved away from its pacifist stance. Clearly, this was a wedding of church and government unknown in previous times. That church-state union became a powerful and eventually destructive and corrupt alliance. The most horrifying illustration of this corrupt alliance came with the bloody Crusades in the Dark Ages.

## Doing Church: Baptist Style

Throughout history many discoveries or recoveries in one area of life came about because of ferment and stirring in other dimensions of life. Although Baptists got our start in seventeenth-century England, England was not isolated and unaffected by what was happening on the European continent. Look at what happened in seventeenth-century England. Politically, civil war erupted. Socially, the struggle for the rights of the common person occurred. Economically, it was the beginning of the industrial age. And culturally, it was the century of Shakespeare and Milton.

While some spiritual reformation of the established church had taken place in the sixteenth century, many felt it had not gone far enough. Baptists were among those dissenters who wanted further reform. They recovered the insight and understanding that the baptism practiced by the apostles was believer's baptism. Request for baptism, Baptists said, was the responsibility and privilege of individual choice, evidence of the priesthood of all believers. We Baptists continue this practice today. Individuals, through their faith experience, encounter God, request to be baptized as an expression of that faith, and promise to serve as a priest of Christ.

The recovery of the biblical principle and teaching of the priesthood of all believers has practical applications. This principle impacts the Baptist vision of Christianity and permeates how Baptists do church.

First, the way Baptists do church means that every individual has direct access to God. Each person is created by God in the image of God. Each person is of equal importance to God. Geographical location, social status, racial identity, educational development, economic standing, vocational choice, and gender identity have no impact, effect, or influence with God. With God there is neither Jew nor Greek, neither slave nor free, neither male nor female (Gal 3:28). All are of equal importance to God, and all have equal access to God. Every individual can approach God and communicate with God about needs, desires, hurts, joys, and celebrations.

Second, the way Baptists do church means that we can be and often are priests to each other. Just as the spirit and presence of God dwelled in Jesus of Nazareth, so God's spirit and presence dwells in each of our lives. Whenever we care for another, love another, empathize with another, listen to the pain and agony and struggle of another, we are priesting them, sharing and carrying their struggles and burdens with them.

Third, the way Baptists do church means that every person has the ability and the right under God's guidance to read, study, interpret, and apply Scripture. Every person is inspired by God. The word inspire means "breathe into." God breathes life, insight, and understanding into every individual. As a result uniform interpretations of passages of Scripture seldom occur. Diverse interpretations, of course, create tension between people. Through Christian dialogue, however, we often share understanding and appreciation for the other's interpretation and point of view. The priesthood of all believers gained popularity with the development of the printing press, resulting in greater access to the printed material, especially the opportunity to read Scripture.

Fourth, the way Baptists do church supports the freedom of the individual to seek out a congregation of which to be a part. People are not assigned a congregation according to the location of the congregation and the residence of the person. Rather, the individual is free to search for a congregation, and a congregation is free to invite and encourage people to become a part of the congregation. Some of these ideas may seem elementary and of no consequence. They are so commonplace that we take them for granted. However, the recovery of the principle of the priesthood of all believers in the seventeenth and eighteenth centuries made these things possible and brought about radical change in the way people did church.

Fifth, the way Baptists do church means that every member of a congregation is of equal value and importance to God and to the congregation. Each member has the right and responsibility to support and express views and opinions about the ministry of the congregation and vote on matters in business meetings that pertain to the life ar.d ministry of the congregation. The priesthood of believers brought about significant change in the way many people did church. A logical result of the priesthood of all believers is a congregational style of decision-making. If individuals are free and responsible, then congregations made up of those individuals become free to make decisions about themselves that determine the way they do ministry. A congregational style of church decision-making ensued. This was different from having an archbishop or a pope make decisions and trickle them down to the people through the hierarchy of bishops and priests.

Sixth, the way Baptists do church leads to the autonomy of the local congregation. In Baptist life, each congregation is responsible for itself. It raises its own funds for ministry; it chooses the resource materials it will use such as Sunday school literature and hymnals; it decides on the type of leadership structure it will have—deacons, organizations, and committees. The local congregation decides on who will be eligible for leadership positions. Some Baptist congregations strongly support women and men in all areas of leadership. Some Baptist congregations, however, strongly disagree with this approach and understanding.

With the autonomy of the local congregation, the local congregation decides on the staff it needs and develops those positions accordingly. The local congregation searches for and invites staff to join it in its ministry. All Baptist churches exercise this process periodically. It enables them to do a national, or international, search for staff. The local congregation develops its own style of worship and programs of ministry. Although there will be similarities to other congregations, each congregation will have its own flavor woven into its specific ministry.

Also, as a result of the way Baptists do church, no one Baptist ever speaks for other Baptists. Only in matters where a group has taken action by vote and one is reporting that action does one ever speak for others. For example, a Baptist pastor has opinions and views on a variety of issues. Because of the importance of freedom and liberty to Baptists, that pastor can express personal views and opinions when and where the pastor wants. Yet, they are the pastor's views and not the views of the congregation with whom the pastor serves. Many people, especially in other denominations, have great difficulty understanding this concept. When Baptist individuals speak, they are wise to keep comments in the first person singular. The opinions are the individual's. She or he speaks for no one else.

Back in 1995, the president and executive committee of the Southern Baptist Convention (SBC) issued a statement opposing a nominee for the position of surgeon general of the United States. They claimed they were speaking for fifteen million Southern Baptists. Many Southern Baptists, however, disagreed with the statement. President Bill Clinton and Vice President Al Gore are Southern Baptists, and they certainly had a different view of the nomination than did the president and the executive committee of the SBC. Certainly the members of the SBC executive committee and the SBC president had every right to be opposed to the nominee. However, they were wrong to imply that they were speaking for Baptists other than themselves. The way Baptists do church clearly underscores respect for the individual's judgment in matters of faith.

Likewise, many people, especially reporters and people from other denominations, have had difficulty understanding why representatives from local Baptist churches to Baptist conventions insist on being called "messengers" rather than "delegates." Once again the way Baptists do church is involved. People are elected as messengers from congregations, but they are not instructed by their congregations on how to vote on issues or candidates. Rather, individual messengers are expected to attend the meetings, use their unique gifts and abilities, make their personal decisions, and vote accordingly on items of business. It is not unusual, therefore, for two Baptists from the same congregation to attend a convention and vote opposite of each other on issues or candidates.

More than thirty years ago Frank Mead identified in his *Handbook of Denominations in the Untied States* twenty-seven different Baptist denominations in this country.[1] Several more splinters have occurred since the publication of that book. Here are the names of a few of the Baptist denominations: National Baptists, Missionary Baptists, Primitive Baptists, Southern Baptists, American Baptists U.S.A., Progressive National Baptists, Hardshell Baptists, Seventh-Day Baptists, and Two-Seed-in-the-Spirit Predestinarian Baptists.

Sometimes the name of a congregation reflects conflict or struggle in that congregation's history. In my hometown many years ago, a major disagreement occurred among the members of the First Baptist Church. Eventually, several members left that congregation, formed another church, purchased property across the street from First Baptist, and named their congregation Immanuel Baptist Church. "Immanuel" means "God with us." Making a statement for posterity, they were saying that God is with us and not with First Baptist! I have been a member of both congregations, perhaps to guarantee that I was a member of the one God was with!

From their beginning in the early 1600s, freedom has been an essential, non-negotiable issue for Baptists. Freedom has been fleshed out in the way Baptists do church. It has implications in the individual's life because of the priesthood of all believers and in the life of the congregation because of local church autonomy. As contemporary Baptists we have inherited our freedom principle from religious ancestors who insisted on it even in the face of ridicule and persecution. Baptists are stewards of freedom!

William B. Lipphard noted in his book *Fifty Years an Editor* that he liked the pastoral security of the Methodist Church, the Presbyterian form of church government, and much of the ritualism of the Episcopal Church. Then he added:

> In one realm of religious experience the Baptists are admittedly different. This is the realm of freedom. As understood and proclaimed by Baptists throughout their history, religion is a personal relationship between the human soul and God. Into this relationship nothing may intrude. . . . Liberty of conscience, freedom from creedal bondage, freedom of

doctrinal interpretation, and local church independence—these constitute Baptist ecclesiastical democracy. . . . Such freedom a Baptist not only insists on for himself, but also grants to all others, and in fact demands for them.[2]

Freedom! It has so much to do with the way Baptists do church. Will you pledge yourself to keeping it alive today? Will you nourish and protect it? Demand it for others? And will you utilize it for yourself within a local congregation of believers?

# Notes

[1]Frank S. Mead, *Handbook of Denominations in the United States* (Nashville: Abingdon, 1961) 32.

[2]William B. Lipphard, cited in O. K. and Marjorie Armstrong, *The Indomitable Baptists* (New York: Doubleday, 1967) 372.

# Prepare the Way of the Lord

## *Wallace Charles Smith*

In those days John the Baptist appeared in the wilderness of Judea, proclaiming, "Repent, for the kingdom of heaven has come near." This is the one of whom the prophet Isaiah spoke when he said, "The voice of one crying out in the wilderness: 'Prepare the way of the Lord, make his paths straight.' " Now John wore clothing of camel's hair with a leather belt around his waist, and his food was locusts and wild honey. Then the people of Jerusalem and all Judea were going out to him, and all the region along the Jordan, and they were baptized by him in the river Jordan, confessing their sins.

But when he saw many Pharisees and Sadducees coming for baptism, he said to them, "You brood of vipers! Who warned you to flee from the wrath to come? Bear fruit worthy of repentance. Do not presume to say to yourselves, 'We have Abraham as our ancestor'; for I tell you, God is able from these stones to raise up children to Abraham. Even now the ax is lying at the root of the trees; every tree therefore that does not bear good fruit is cut down and thrown into the fire." (Matt 3:1-10)

On this day, the wilderness repentance preaching of John had attracted a motley and oddly configured crowd. There was the usual assortment of the poor, the afflicted, and the broken. Those who were the dirty and unwashed, the unscrubbed and poorly kept arrived that day at the Jordan as usual. These beaten, broken pilgrims came with penitent minds. They fully understood the need for turning away from the evils of this world and toward a Lord of hope and sovereign of possibilities. Those poor persons appreciated the necessity for a fresh start and an altered life's course. The 1960s songwriter poet Bob Dylan wrote, "When you ain't got nothing, you got nothing to lose." Those despised, disenfranchised, denigrated members of Jewish society who sought John at the Jordan fully understood that they had to lay their all on the altar. They had nowhere else to turn.

But there was another crowd. They seemed to be attempting to sneak into the frat. They represented another mind-set. Among the crowd that day were scribes and Pharisees. The text says, "When he [John] saw many Pharisees and Sadducees coming for baptism, he said to them, 'You brood of vipers! Who warned you to flee from the wrath to come?' " This was surely uncourteous behavior on John's part. He must not have known what the scribes and Pharisees were. These separated, saintly, and selected ones functioned as the *crème de la crème*. They were the pillars in a crumbling world. They were the rock in societal shifting sand.

They held together the unraveling fabric of a world threadbare from oppression. For 400 years there had been no prophets. For 400 years the demanding, troubling, trying commands of Isaiah, Jeremiah, and Ezekiel had been quieter than moonlight on a snowfall. For 4,000 decades the people had endured without a word from the Lord, and in that absence the scribes and Pharisees had been the spiritual and religious wood that had kept the fires of righteous fervor burning.

Yet, it was to the already religious, heretofore-faithful, to-date spiritual crowd that John cried out, "Repent for the kingdom is near." Not that he was not calling for Roman soldiers, the tax gatherers, and the prostitutes to alter their courses, but he was leaning on the saved, satisfied, and sanctified who believed that claiming Abraham as their father would ensure that their souls were safe. One problem self-righteous people possess is a confusion about the fact that they too are in the wilderness.

We Baptists subscribe to what is commonly known as "the Protestant Principle." The reformers of the Protestant Reformation utilized a Latin phrase, *ecclesia semper reformanda*, to describe this principle: the church always being reformed. Repentance is the avenue to reformation, both without and within the church. Sometimes we call it revival. Sometimes we call it renewal. Sometimes we call it reformation. John simply called it repentance.

So here was this prophet in tailored camel hair delivering a message to every man, woman, boy, and girl. Regardless of how long we have been in church, we've got some wilderness to deal with. In spite of our upbringing, training, or competence; no matter what committees we have worked on, boards we have served, or contributions we have offered, attending church is the time when we should take stock of our souls, selves, and spirits and work as adequately, vigilantly, and valiantly on our relationship with God. Repent for the kingdom of heaven is at hand.

All we—not some—like sheep have gone astray. Our church conducted a survey two years ago and discovered that some people do not attend church school because they feel they do not need to. All we like sheep have gone astray.

What is repentance? In the Greek it is *metanoia*, meaning turning. Repentance requires a changing of mind. Repentance mandates an altering of priorities. Repentance demands a reversal from sin and a redirection toward God. Recently I watched a football contest waged on the gridiron of one of the nation's prestigious schools. The quarterback ran toward right end. The flanker came back, took the ball, and along with the blockers ran toward left end. In football this play is called a reverse. In theology one calls it repentance.

## What Is Repentance?

Deuteronomy states:

> When all these things have happened to you, the blessings and the curses that I have set before you, if you call them to mind . . . and return to the Lord your God, . . . then the Lord your God will restore your fortunes and have compassion on you, gathering you again from all the peoples among whom the Lord your God has scattered you. (30:1-3)

That's repentance.
Isaiah declared:

> Seek the Lord while He may be found, call upon him while He is near;
> Let the wicked forsake their way, and the unrighteous their thoughts; let them return to the Lord, that he may have mercy on them, and to our God, and for he will abundantly pardon. (Isa 55:6-7)

That's repentance.
The Chronicler declared:

> If my people who are called by my name will humble themselves, pray, seek my face, and turn from their wicked ways, then will I hear from heaven, and will forgive their sin and heal their land. (2 Chron 7:14)

That's repentance.
Repentance is a soul's maintenance plan. It is a matter administered not by Mr. Goodwrench but by Mr. Good News.
At prescribed intervals the most efficient and effective automobiles must be brought to an authorized establishment; the entire timing analyzed; the grease in the oil supply replaced with fresh lubricant; the fluids and charges examined, monitored, and reinvigorated. That's routine maintenance. Periodically, the heart must return to its designer, the soul placed on a lift and scrutinized, the grime of

disobedience and inauthenticity replaced by fresh mercy and grace fluids. That's repentance.

Some of us get nowhere because we have been driving unmaintained souls, poorly serviced spirits, improperly diagnosed hearts. Not just occasionally, but constantly we must repent. We must ask God to forgive us for the sins of omission, that which happened and which we did not intend, and of commission, that which we meant to do. Repentance is asking mercy for each soul we wound. Repentance is sending for forgiveness for all the hearts we break. Repentance begs for grace when we through our insensitivities destroy lives, destruct homes, and wound the innocent.

We do not have to take a wrecking ball and knock down someone's house. Whenever an uncharitable thought delivers destruction, repentance is required. Each unkind word that carries venom calls for repentance. All unsympathetic behavior that dips the arrows of darkness into the poison of destruction mandates repentance.

All we like sheep have gone astray. John said to us all—rich, poor, young, old, religious, irreligious—"I am the voice of one crying . . . in the wilderness, . . . in the long night of dislocation, . . . in the creeping process of aging, . . . in the bitter realities of loneliness, . . . against the ravaging, raging fires of uncertainty and doubt. . . . It is not position or influence in the church that saves you. Repent for the kingdom of Heaven is at hand."

Repent, John preached, for the kingdom of God looms as an imminent reality. What is repentance? It is denying the limitations of the past and then defining ourselves along kingdom values.

Deny the limitations of the past! Some persons cannot achieve, accomplish, or succeed because they are carrying too much "I can't" around with them. Many persons have mathematics phobias. Someone told us in eighth or ninth grade that we could not do math, and we have been afraid to try it since. Repentance is a turning away from the old ways and turning toward God. Regardless of the limitations life has placed upon us, repentance instructs us to deny the past's power to define. "Build your hopes on things eternal; hold to God's unchanging hand."

If the power of the past laughed at you because you were too short, made fun of you because you were tall, didn't select you for the team because you were overweight, beat you up because you were skinny, denied you work because you were black, asked you to take notes because you were a woman, told you your worship was ignorant and non-liturgical because you were Baptist, said your intelligence was suspect because you believe there is a God, turn from the past's power and allow yourself to be defined by the spirit of God. That's what repentance will do. Repentance will set you free.

Some of those same negative definitions caused us to develop destructive lifestyles. Because somebody beat us up, we bought a gun. If we were told we were unattractive, we became promiscuous. If we were never loved, we wounded and hurt others. There is no definition placed on us by the world that we cannot overcome if we are willing to redefine ourselves by the spirit of God.

John called the scribes and Pharisees vipers because they wanted to sneak into the kingdom. They wanted solutions without repentance. We must turn our backs on those old ancient devils who define us and accept new names, new identities, new lifestyles.

A cube of ice on a hot day will survive only for a short period of time. Whatever we have permitted to be our definition cannot last if it is contrary to the will of God. Murdering people with our words cannot exist in a kingdom of truth. Treating our bodies and others uncharitably and irresponsibly will not stand in a new world marked by accountability.

Repentance is breaking free from the definitions of the past and turning toward our God. Repentance is also when we understand that salvation comes at the intersection of judgment and hope. John said the axe is laid to the root of the tree, not just the branches. Jesus spoke of the patient owner who waited while the keeper of the garden took another year to work on an unproductive fruit tree—pruning, fertilizing, watering. But after clippers comes the axe. God will set this world on fire. A day of judgment shall come. We must be reminded that we cannot dillydally, play, and believe that we have limitless time. We may leave worship at the church house and not make it back next Sunday. Repentance comes to church when we realize we must turn from our destructive pathways.

One more bottle of booze could be the one that will cause our heart valves to shut down precipitously. Then in the hospital, we will find ourselves unable to maintain sovereignty over our bodies. Doctors in white coats will be explaining how a major vein from the leg must be removed, our breastbones and ribs broken, the heart opened wide, restitched by strangers who will leave us with a survival chance of 50/50. The axe will be laid to the root of the tree.

Now is the day of salvation: when we have lied and fabricated to cover up, and then we go one prevarication over the line; people begin comparing notes of what we said to whom; before we can stop the out-of-control spark that we tried to hide looses itself and runs unchecked like a raging fire until our reputations are ruined, our families destroyed, and our futures clouded. The axe will be laid to the root of the tree.

Or, there may be times when aching loneliness drives one to multiple partners, illicit contacts, immoral intersections. Our nights may be filled with strangers' embraces as we attempt to drive off the pain of empty existence, but then the diagnosis returns HIV positive. The axe will be laid to the root of the tree.

All of life is a rehearsal for eternity. Some will make the crew; some will not. Seek God while God can be found. On the Niagara River for years there was a sign just at the Falls that said, *Past redemption point.* How many masked opportunities! How long will we deny the nobility in our souls and wallow with the swine, fraternize with worms and maggots, accept vipers and vermin as our roommates? The axe is laid to the root of the tree. Now is the day of Salvation. Prepare ye the way of the Lord.

While vacationing in Maui a few years ago, we took a motor tour on a road that was marked hazardous ahead, proceed at your own risk. We did not take it, but others did. We were told that, although the road appears perfect upon debarkation—wide, well paved, brightly lit—after a time, it begins to narrow. The surface is not as well kept; the blacktop turns to concrete, broken and crooked. After a while, the road becomes gravel, finally dirt. On muddy days, only those with four-wheel drive have any hope of safe passage.

But know this, when it pertains to matters of the heart, there has never been a four-wheel drive vehicle that safely negotiates the roadway to destruction. This hell-bound highway is broad and beautiful when we begin. Copious fellow travelers provide plenteous accompaniment on the path. But soon the road narrows. The street underneath cracks. The going crosses into treachery. The amount of little white powder it once took to get high is no longer sufficient. More and more drugs produce dwindling results. We spend more money we don't have. Credit cards are run up. Gambling bills are incurred, bank accounts looted. The axe is laid to the root of the tree.

John the Baptist said the road ahead is filled with destruction; death awaits along with unspeakable agony, tragedy, heartbreak. But there is a road sign warning us, and that is the hope. Take this exit, or drive untold miles out of the way. The warning sign is the hope: Prepare ye the way of the Lord. Make straight in the desert a highway for our God. Repent for the kingdom of heaven is at hand.

# A Church, Open

## Daniel Carro

For the love of Christ urges us on, because we are convinced that one has died for all; therefore all have died. And he died for all, so that those who live might live no longer for themselves, but for him who died and was raised for them.

From now on, therefore, we regard no one from a human point of view; even though we once knew Christ from a human point of view, we know him no longer in that way. So if anyone is in Christ, there is a new creation: everything old has passed away; see, everything has become new! All this is from God, who reconciled us to himself through Christ, and has given us the ministry of reconciliation; that is, in Christ God was reconciling the world to himself, not counting their trespasses against them, and entrusting the message of reconciliation to us. So we are ambassadors for Christ, since God is making his appeal through us; we entreat you on behalf of Christ, be reconciled to God. (2 Cor 5:14-20)

The future of the church is not the domain of futurology. Neither is it a matter of playing the prophet in order to predict the church of tomorrow. But unless we identify certain directions for the church today, we will not know what conditions will exist for the church of tomorrow. The church of tomorrow depends entirely on the strategies we follow today. What we do today will determine the shape of the church tomorrow.

The church of the future should follow a biblical pattern of openness. The church needs to be open. There never was, there is not now, and there never will be a *closed* church. A closed church is a contradiction in terms. Whatever else the church of Jesus Christ is, it is open. Wide open!

In Matthew 18:18, Jesus says: "Truly I tell you, whatever you bind on earth will be bound in heaven, and whatever you loose on earth will be loosed in heaven." Earlier Jesus had said something similar to Peter in Matthew 16:19: "I will give you the keys of the kingdom of heaven, and whatever you bind . . . " Jesus also said to him that "the gates of Hades will not prevail against" the church (Matt 16:18).

Jesus spoke of keys. He spoke of binding and unbinding, of closing and opening, and he spoke of some gates that would never be closed against the church. Indeed, he referred to the disciples' personal responsibility in the future of the church. Likewise, Baptist Christians around the world are responsible for the future Baptist way of being church.

At the British Cemetery in Buenos Aires is the tomb of Reverend Don Santiago Canclini, one of Argentina's greatest Baptist pastors ever. From that grave, Don Santiago asks—through the words of a poem engraved on a plaque—what maybe only God can truly ask: "How is the race doing, carrier of the torch? Is the flame alive? Is the faith still burning?"

We who are the church today carry the torch of the Christian faith. Our ancestors are now gone. Our successors have not yet come. In the words of the popular song: "*We* are the world, *We* are the people, *We* are the ones to make a better world, so let's start giving." *We* are the future of the church!

In every authentic effort at being church, disciples hear a call to personal responsibility, involvement, and commitment in the life of the church. With the obligation comes risk, the risk that the flame could flicker, that our faith would not burn as brightly as it burned in the hearts of our forerunners. We run the risk of apathy and indolence, even the risk of losing the race.

If we are to have a dynamic church, Christians need to answer the questions: What kind of church do we want to have? How do we envision the future of our way of being the church? Towards where do we direct our steps when we speak about the church of the future?

From where I live in South America, I see the crucial issue for the future of the church as *openness*. We Baptists, today and in the future, must walk together towards an authentically open church. Specifically, what does openness in the church mean? What kind of church is an open church? What are the salient features of a church that is open?

First, we need to walk together towards a church open to God's influx. Paul states something of his understanding of the nature of the church in 2 Corinthians 5:14-20. He begins by saying that "the love of Christ urges us on" (5:14). The word translated *urges* means to constrain, to compel, or to require. It is to command; it is to demand. The church is motivated by the love of Christ; nothing else compels our lives or drives our commitments. Christ's love is our primary impetus in the mission of the church.

Influx! The image is a flood, an inundation, an invasion. The word signals an inflowing power from somewhere else. God is our flood! Jesus Christ is our inflow. The Holy Spirit controls and inundates our lives. In other words, the gates of the church should be wide open to a transcendent invasion of unspeakable love. Our minds and hearts are to be open to receive God's influx.

John said of Jesus: "He came to what was his own, and his own people did not accept him" (John 1:11). Many times I fear that the same thing could happen to our Baptist way of being church in the world. What if Jesus comes to us to do his business? What if, instead of receiving him with joy and cheerfulness, we reject him? Could it happen to those of us within the church? We know it could happen outside the church? Might it also happen inside church?

Jesus is a friend issuing an invitation. "Follow me," he says. But if we do not follow, might this friend leave us to ourselves? What would become of us in the church without Jesus? Where else would we get power to do the task? As Peter said: "Lord, to whom can we go?" (John 6:68).

Even when we turn to God, we will have to remember that God is unpredictable and uncontrollable. Christians cannot put limits to God's activity according to denominational parameters. God's ways are not our ways; God's thinking is not our thinking. God is spirit, and the spirit blows where it chooses. God's freedom cannot be confined by conditions imposed by human beings.

The great German theologian Hans Küng wrote eloquently about the freedom of God to his Catholic community:

> The Holy Spirit is no other than God himself. The Spirit works *where* he wills. The Spirit of God cannot be restricted in effectiveness by the Church. The Spirit works not only from above but very decisively from below. He works not only in church ministries, but where he wills: in the whole people of God. He works not only in the Holy City but where he wills: in all churches and the one Church. He works not only in the Catholic Church but where he wills: in the whole of Christendom. And finally, he works not only in Christendom but again where he wills: in the whole world.[1]

We Baptists need that strong word from Küng. Instead of trying to control God, we need to yield ourselves to God's control. We need Christ's power and love in the church. "Listen! I am standing at the door, knocking; if you hear my voice and open the door, I will come in to you, and eat with you, and you with me" (Rev 3:20). We need a church, open to a divine influx.

Second, we need to walk together towards a church open to its interior world. Paul continues by saying that Christ "died for all, so that those who live might live no longer for themselves, but for him who died and who was raised for them" (2 Cor 5:15). Also to the Philippians Paul wrote: "Let each of you look not to your own interests, but to the interests of others" (Phil 2:4).

A church open to its interior world is a church open to all of its members, regardless of class, gender, color, or previous religious background. It is a church open to all voices, interests, and points of view. Next to closing itself off to God's spirit, the church does itself the greatest harm by closing itself off to the whole of its membership. When a church centers on a ruling pastor, a dominant group, or a controlling bureaucracy—that is the beginning of the end of God's church in that place.

The old Latin saying goes: *Vox populi, vox Dei,* "people's voice, God's voice." The church is the people! The church is not the pastor, the deacons, or the ruling leadership. Leadership is always demanded by the church. But the leaders must always remember their origins. In Baptist churches leaders and their authority come from the people. Responsible *for* the people, the leaders are accountable *to* the people. Every church constantly needs to combat against the sectarian mentality, against the shrinking of the vision, against the domination of the few in the interior church world.

There is no way for churches to be open to God if they close out the human gifts within themselves. The church has to be open to all. Each member of the body of Christ must have space within the church, and each must have a place for mission and ministry in Christ's name.

Regrettably, Baptist churches are not exempt from the tendency toward authoritarianism. That authoritarianism comes to Baptists in two forms, one pastoral, the other congregational. At times, an unhealthy pastoral domination of the church appears in Baptist life. At other times, a disrespect for the ministry manifests in congregational tyranny of its leadership. We need a sound combination of ministerial leadership and congregational authority, a balance of responsibilities and benefits, a fit combination of pastoral participation and congregational involvement. We need churches for the future that are open to all people within the church.

Third, we need to walk together towards a church open to the exterior world. Paul said, "All this is from God, who reconciled us to himself through Christ, and has given us the ministry of reconciliation" (2 Cor 5:18).

If the church today looks forward to a bright future, it must open itself to the exterior world in a twofold way. The church must be open to testimony and open to service. A silent Christian is a Christian who is closed to the exterior world. A Christian who is not involved in service is closed to the possibilities that God has for the world where that Christian lives. Many people are willing to be a part of the church. Those of us in the church must open the church for them; we have to facilitate the entrance of willing believers into the kingdom, instead of obstructing their participation in the authentic church.

Augustine used to say that there were two kinds of people in the church. There are those who belong *according to the heart*, the believers; and there are those who belong only *according to the body*, that is, those who see participation in the church as only a social commitment. The difference between the two ways of belonging hinges on a confession of Jesus Christ as Lord, both in word and in action.

The church must abandon forever its custom of dividing the world into believers and nonbelievers. A lady in the Ramos Mejia Church (where I am pastor) once introduced a man to me with these words: "Pastor, this is my husband. He is a nonbeliever." Of course, the man never came back again to church. He was a nonbeliever by definition. How can a nonbeliever be converted? Only a believer can be converted. Only a person who already belongs to the body of the church can become a part of its heart.

There is no reason to divide humanity so rigidly between those who are committed members of a church, with all their rights and duties, and those who are hostile or indifferent to the church. The task of the church is not to divide; we are to reconcile. We were not called by God to be ministers of division, but ministers of reconciliation.

Not every person is like the prodigal son. Not all people conform to the image of the young rich ruler. We have to abandon the extremes of profligacy and complacency and take contemporary humanity in its peculiar dimension. We must see our sisters and brothers in the world as they are, and aid their entrance to the church.

Of course, the church cannot be open to the world in which it exists to the degree that it becomes a reflection of it. The church cannot let the world of sin invade its walls; we cannot allow the exterior world to turn us upside down. Rather, it should be exactly the opposite. The task of the church is to turn the exterior world upside down! Such a transformation will hardly be done if the church is not open to the real world. If there is no openness to the world, there is no relation to the world. If there is no relation between the church and the world, there is no ministry of reconciliation. If there is no ministry, there is no reconciliation with God. So the church must be open; no other way exists for the church.

The church today cannot continue to exist in a private or cloistered corner of the world. The church must abdicate forever a ghetto mentality. The ghetto mentality focuses on quantity rather than quality. In a ghetto there is security and authority in numbers. The ghetto survives through a mentality of division and provincialism. The church has a very different calling.

In the church there may be a security in numbers, but the church is more than that. We may be many, but the church exists not through division and provincialism, but through a willingness to break down the old stereotypes that divide and isolate. If the church is to be authentic, it must pursue real answers for contemporary questions. Reconciliation is only possible when the church listens intently to the questions of the world in which the church exists.

This is the balance that has to be pursued. How to have a church open to the exterior world in testimony and in service through a new and singular experiment without converting the church in a public bazaar where everything and everybody is useful and valid because everything, even the gospel of Jesus Christ, is put on sale at the market price. We need a church, open to the exterior world.

Last of all, we need to walk together towards a church open to a future of hope in Christ. Paul ends his argument saying: "In Christ God was reconciling the world to himself, not counting their trespasses against them" (2 Cor 5:19).

In Christ there is hope. Christ is the future hope for the whole world. God is not against the world; God is reconciling the world to Himself in and through Jesus Christ. Every time and everywhere that any person is personally or communally reconciled with God, hope is still alive. We Christians do not have to live in despair. Ours is not a philosophy of nihilism. We have hope. We are a people of hope. The church is God's agent of reconciliation in a world divided in every conceivable way. But if we preach Christ, we preach hope for the world.

The German theologian Jürgen Moltmann directed our attention towards a "theology of hope." He said,

> The new life of regeneration is determined by an inclusive hope. It is not an exclusive hope according to which one just wish to save oneself and let the rest of the world go to hell. The soliciting mercy of God makes this new Creation of the world, which becomes the Kingdom of his

glory, to begin right now in the individual Christian and in the Christian community through the gifts of the Holy Spirit. This Spirit is nothing more than the strength of this new Creation. Where it works, the process of regeneration of the whole creation begins. Who has been regenerated by the Spirit, live continuously in the hope of the future glory. But s/he lives in the world, with the world, and for the world which is to become the scenario of the glory of God. The regeneration in the Spirit does not isolate man but take him/her into the community with other fellows. It puts every individual into the world fellowship of the Holy Spirit, which is to be poured out upon all flesh.[2]

Our Baptist way of being the church must show the world how to walk in hope. Human beings are creatures that only survive in hope. People do not mature in desperation, but in faith and hope; not in death, but in aspiration of life; not in solitude, but in moments of communion and love. If despair prevailed, everyone would die or kill themselves. But when there is hope, there is salvation. Ideals do not save humanity. Neither do intellect or reason, or a commitment to a cause. The future of humanity and the world relies on hope. Christian hope gives society a new integrative vitality that society did not know otherwise: the life of Christ. Every Christian is a representative of the gospel that transforms people and cultures. The transforming gospel is the hope for the world. The transformation is made manifest in the life of hopeful Christians living in a most hopeless society. We need a church, open to a future of hope.

A church, open. This is what we need. A church, open to God's influx. A church, open to its interior world. A church, open to the exterior world in testimony and service. A church, open to a future of hope.

The church of the future must become great, not only in numbers (which occupies the contemporary mind), but also in quality, in personal and communal betterment, and in diversity of thought and action. Only an open church can become a great church. We need a church, open. Wide open. Each of us has the keys of the kingdom in our hands.

# Notes

[1]Hans Küng, *The Church—Maintained in Truth* (New York: Random House, 1982) 22-24.

[2]Jürgen Moltmann, *Temas para una teologia de la esperanza*, author's English translation.

# To What
# Church Do You Belong?

## William Powell Tuck

As a deer longs for flowing streams, so my soul longs for you, O God.
My soul thirsts for God, for the living God. When shall I come and
behold the face of God? My tears have been my food day and night,
while people say to me continually, "Where is your God?" These things
I remember, as I pour out my soul: how I went with the throng, and led
them in procession to the house of God, with glad shouts and songs of
thanksgiving, a multitude keeping festival. Why are you cast down, O
my soul, and why are you disquieted within me? Hope in God; for I
shall again praise him, my help and my God. My soul is cast down
within me; therefore I remember you from the land of Jordan and of
Hermon, from Mount Mizar. Deep calls to deep at the thunder of your
cataracts; all your waves and your billows have gone over me. By day
the Lord commands his steadfast love, and at night his song is with me,
a prayer to the God of my life. (Ps 42:1-8)

I hope to come to you soon, but I am writing these instructions to you
so that, if I am delayed, you may know how one ought to behave in the
household of God, which is the church of the living God, the pillar and
bulwark of the truth. Without any doubt, the mystery of our religion is
great: He was revealed in flesh, vindicated in spirit, seen by angels, proclaimed among Gentiles, believed in throughout the world, taken up in
glory. (1 Tim 3:14-16)

Driving along the expressway, I noticed a huge billboard that read:
*Attend the church of your choice.* What could be more American than
that? It is almost as American as apple pie. Attend the church of your
choice. America contains more varieties of religious denominations
than Baskin Robbins has ice cream. You have lots of choices. Our ancestors wrote an amendment to our constitution that guaranteed that
freedom: "Congress shall make no law respecting an establishment of
religion, or prohibiting the free exercise thereof." But as good as the
phrase, "Attend the church of your choice," is, something in it dis-
turbs me. Since it bothers me, it may perturb you. Consider some of
the churches available to you in America today.

# The Only Understanding of Truth Church

Some persons belong to The Only Understanding of Truth Church. This church claims it has a special handle on truth. Nobody else has the insight into truth. Members of this church narrow all truth to their own focus. They collect religious truth in propositional form, and anyone who would be a part of *the true church* has to ascribe to their set of beliefs. They assert that not only are their beliefs inerrant and infallible, but so is their interpretation of them. They alone have the truth.

Members of this church are rigid, inflexible, unbending, and uncompromising. All other interpretations are elbowed out in the name of their truth claims. After all, if you have the truth, as they claim to have it, how dare anyone differ with their view of God or how we are to live as God's children. Persons in this church show no patience with religions such as Hinduism, Buddhism, Confucianism, or Taoism that allow tolerance for the beliefs of others. Their spirit is linked closely with the fundamentalist strains of Islam that react with vindictiveness to destroy any other religious perspective differing from their own. If you do not belong to The Church with the Only Understanding of Truth, then you are an infidel.

This church's heritage reaches back through the centuries and finds its roots in a perversion of ancient Judaism. Israel declared boldly that it was God's only true people. Some among the Jewish people nobly understood this calling in terms of service to the world. But some misunderstood and transformed the calling into an arrogant and privileged status. The latter stressed their chosenness, emphasizing all others' lack of chosenness.

Our Lord encountered members of this church when he came to minister. The scribes and Pharisees belonged to that kind of church and held tenaciously and rigidly to their interpretation of religion. How dare Jesus challenge their interpretation of the truth! They knew they had the only correct knowledge of religious truth, and they helped crucify Jesus because he dared to challenge their understanding of life.

Saul belonged for a while to The Only Understanding of Truth Church. He persecuted the early Christian church and even held the outer garments for the men who stoned Stephen. But when claimed by Christ, Paul immediately disassociated himself from that religious church. Before long, however, he encountered another form of that same kind of church. It stated that unless Christians became Jews (were circumcised), they could not be true Christians. Paul spent his life arguing for a different and more tolerant kind of church.

Down through the centuries, The Only Understanding of Truth Church has sought to dominate and control the beliefs of others. We often think of the members of this church as bigots. Do you know the origin of that word? It comes from a condensation of *by God!* "By God!" these persons assert, "I have got all the truth, and I am going to cram it down your throat, control your thinking, and make everybody else believe just like I do."

The Inquisition sprang from those who belonged to The Only Understanding of Truth Church. When anybody dared differ with established truth, they were put to death. In 1572, Catherine de Medici executed 20,000 French Protestants because they differed with the established church of that day. The pope sent her a letter congratulating her on the Saint Bartholomew's Day massacre. John Wycliffe translated the Scriptures from Latin into English and so outraged the established church that it condemned him to death. While the church condemned him, because of his protection, it could not harm him. After his death, however, the pope had his bones dug up and burned and his ashes cast into a river so he would not have a place of burial.

Do not think, however, that Catholics have a monopoly on intolerance in Christian history. John Calvin, one of the foremost leaders in the Protestant Reformation, executed a Spanish physician, named Servetus, who differed with him on his interpretation of the Trinity. When the Puritans hounded Roger Williams out of Salem Colony in 1636, he promptly founded Providence, Rhode Island, where all persons might have religious freedom.

The Only Understanding of Truth Church is not confined to any one religion or any single expression of Christianity. It cuts across all denominations. Freedom-loving Baptists, of all persons, one might think, would never be members of that church. Two of the foundational concepts in Baptists' beliefs are the priesthood of all believers and religious tolerance. But, not too many generations ago, Crawford Toy and William Whitsitt had to resign their positions at Southern Baptist Theological Seminary because they were considered heretics when they employed critical tools in their understanding of the Bible.

Now today, several generations later, members of The Only Understanding of Truth Church parade across the Baptist denominational landscape once again. Lifting up their banners of truth and engaging in theological witch hunts, they seek to remove professors from seminaries who differ with those who claim to have the only correct understanding of truth. Members of this distorted church unfortunately see truth as finished. God has spoken; but God doesn't continue to speak. According to their view, God simply cannot be at work within the church bringing individuals new and fresh visions of divine will and ways. Truth for them is finished and regulated.

When I was a pastor in Virginia, I came in from lunch one day and saw two ministers engaged in conversation with my secretary. It was obvious that they were preachers. They were dressed in the uniforms that quickly convey that message, and they spoke with stained-glass voices. I spoke to them as I came in the door, and started to move on past them since I did not recognize them. Suddenly, I realized that they were theologically attacking my secretary. They were seeking to convert her. You need to know that she was a fine Episcopalian. She had been a secretary at the church for years, and I had never tried to proselytize her into the Baptist fold. She attended her own church and worshiped faithfully. So I turned to them and said: "Pardon me, but I don't believe I like the way you are talking to my secretary." They, then, turned to me and began to attack me. "Do you believe such and such?" I had an appointment in a few minutes, and I said: "Friend, I would love to have time to debate with you about this theological issue, but I do not. I know 'whom I have believed,' and I am very happy in my faith, and I hope you are in yours. God bless you. I have to go and do some other work."

Several weeks later one of our church members told me that she went to another city to attend a funeral service. The ministers, in that funeral service of all places, stood before the grieving family and declared: "You wouldn't believe what a preacher up in Harrisonburg told me that he doesn't believe." Then he began to list a long series of things that he said I did not believe. Well, it so happened that I did believe those things he said I denied. But the worst part is that he had never discussed any of those beliefs with me to know whether I believed them or not. If you refused to dialogue with him about his beliefs, he assumed you did not believe as you should. He already had the right belief, and any who did not agree was a heretic. We have too many of these theological witch hunters in Baptist life today who belong to The Only Understanding of Truth Church. They exclude rather than include sisters and brothers of the faith.

In his novel *Julian*, Gore Vidal depicts a scene in the fourth century where the Roman emperor Julian replaced Christianity as the official religion and restored the pagan gods. He considered Christianity dangerous and immoral. One of his aides asked him if he was going to outlaw Christianity as Christianity outlawed the worship of the pagan gods and persecute the Christians as the Christians had persecuted those who worshiped the pagan gods? "No, leave them alone," Julian said in effect. "I think sooner or later the Christians will kill off each other."

What an indictment on the church! We will kill each other off! Did you read the quip by Henlee Barnette? "Have you noticed that when a minister begins to play God, he winds up acting like the devil?" When anybody thinks they have the only truth about God, they are dangerous. Unfortunately, too many people belong to this church.

## The Warm Feeling, Friendly, Everybody-Always-Happy, Noncontroversial, Easygoing, Crowd-Pleasing, Entertaining Church

Others hold membership in another church. They belong to The Warm Feeling, Friendly, Everybody-Always-Happy, Noncontroversial, Easygoing, Crowd-Pleasing, Entertaining Church. Its membership is widespread. People join this church basically to get their own individual needs satisfied. It offers them exactly what they want. Whatever they want, the church is obligated to provide it. This church offers programs for every age—children, teenagers, singles, young adults, and older adults. Whatever people desire, it is satisfied by this church.

This church never engages in anything controversial. It doesn't want anything to create disturbances or disharmony. Everything is done to make people feel good and be happy. Nothing controversial is ever allowed or mentioned. The pulpit of this church spews simple sermons for satisfied minds. Preached here are pleasing, peaceful platitudes for pious, placid persons. Disturbances, moral or otherwise, are not tolerated.

Worship services are planned primarily for their entertainment value. The more the spectators feel they have been entertained, the more they think they have worshiped. When they leave this church, they want to feel warm and cozy inside. The worship of Almighty God becomes the theological equivalent of a Lawrence Welk *Variety Hour* with the humor and theological depth of *Hee Haw* and the excitement of a NCAA basketball championship. This church focuses primarily on entertaining us and making us feel satisfied.

In a *New Yorker* cartoon, a church is depicted with its front doors open and the congregation exiting after the worship hour. Everybody is fighting and arguing with each other. One woman is pictured hitting the minister over the head with her umbrella. A man and woman are passing by and observing this conflict. She says to him, "Goodness, I wonder what word of comfort for a troubled world the minister shared today."

Sometimes the word of God is not "Comfort ye, comfort ye my people." The word of God may need to cut into our lives with sharpness, addressing us with a "Thus saith the Lord." God's word may come to us in crass, rustic language, declaring us sinners in need of radical repentance. What entertainment do you see in the crucifixion of Jesus? And where is the warmth in Jesus' radical call to discipleship with the attendant command to go into the world and lay down your life for the cause of love?

Christ's teachings contain a sharp flint side. Christian discipleship has a sandpaper edge to it. The words of Jesus are often pointed, not always focusing on what people want but on what they need. Rather than constantly comforting his hearers, Jesus often challenged the comfortable. The prophetic words of Christ summon us to walk the more difficult way and not be content with the comforts of life.

The grace of Christ, as Bonhoeffer reminded us in word and life, is never cheap. The church of Jesus Christ aims not merely to make us feel good or tranquil or to provide us a peaceful escape from the world. The danger of a church obsessed with crowd-pleasing, entertaining, or peace-of-mind theology is that it may become a church of our own creation and not the church for which Christ died. The membership of this church is large and growing today.

## The Traditional, Established, Routine, Well-Regulated, Standard, Status Quo Church of the Satisfied God

Others in America want to be members of The Traditional, Established, Routine, Well-Regulated, Standard, Status Quo Church of the Satisfied God. This church is steeped in tradition. Everything it does reaches back to ancient times. It carefully seeks to carry forward its traditions from generation to generation. There is, of course, nothing wrong with traditions, rightly used.

But in this church where change is the enemy, routine slowly becomes rut. The sameness of worship practices becomes so familiar that variety is unheard of. Set in its way, this traditional church never expects anything different to happen. God has spoken in the past, but does not continue to speak today. In this church people want nothing disturbed, nothing touched, nothing changed. They have their routine. They walk in it and do not want someone fiddling with their establishment. "Don't fix it when it ain't broke," they say. Traditions become unchangeable laws of God.

In California, there is a store called the Surprise Shop. Go into that shop, and you discover all kinds of novel items. People are happily surprised with the many and varied possibilities for purchasing. Shouldn't the church be like the Surprise Shop, open to the Holy Spirit who is breathing its new life into the church? God's church can never be totally routine, if God is constantly breaking in to surprise it with new possibilities.

Several years ago I heard Krister Stendahl, the former dean at Harvard Divinity School, speak at a church conference. He said that the contemporary church probably has all of the same problems and difficulties of the early Corinthian church except one. The church at Corinth did not suffer from the sin of dullness! Sometimes the church, regulated by its traditions, becomes deadly dull. The danger here is apathy! The danger here is a cavalier approach to eternal matters! The danger here is indifference to God's will!

A problem arose in a church in Scotland because noted poet Robert Burns lay buried in the church cemetery. Everybody in that community wanted to be buried in that cemetery with Robert Burns. Seeking to deal with the problem, the church posted a sign on the cemetery fence: "This cemetery is reserved for the dead now living in this parish."

Too often the traditional church is composed of the dead now living in it. They have no sense of aliveness to the spirit of God that is trying to break in with the freshness of God's presence and give the church new directions, new hopes, and new ways of being church. The traditional church is dead to God's spirit and very content with where it is. It is self-satisfied. It has already toed the correct line, so why disturb anything.

A wonderful story comes out of the freezing Arctic. Once the weather was so cold there that the flames on the candles froze! The explorers reached over, broke off the frozen flame of the candles, and turned them into charms. The flaming power of God, which has ignited the church in the past, has often been turned into ornaments and charms today. Many now wear a cross around their necks. The great symbols of the church have been turned into ornaments. The flaming power of Christ is not present in this kind of church. A contented church loses its power, ceases to be salt, light, and leaven in the world for Christ. The church can never by contented with where it is. God forever nudges it forward into what it can be as it is remade in God's image.

## The Visionary, Pioneering Church of the Living God

Another church, thank God, exists in our land today. It is The Visionary, Pioneering Church of the Living God. This church hears an echo about its mission from the ancient psalmist who cried: "I thirst for the living God." Some scholars believe that the writer of Psalm 42 was a woman. She used the image of a female deer to begin her story. A deer is searching and groping for water. She arrives at a water hole but cannot find water. The waterhole is completely barren, so the deer leaves without satisfying her thirst. A great thirst in this woman's life had not been fulfilled. Maybe taken captive and carried into exile in Egypt, she longed to return and worship with the throngs of Israelites going up to the Jerusalem Temple to worship God. A thirst within her very being was not satisfied in that strange land, and she cried out: "I thirst for the living God."

The cry, "I thirst," is the cry of every man and woman. There is an unconscious longing within each of us. Who among us does not thirst for the presence of God? We long for the divine, knowing that the eternal alone can satisfy our real thirst. We turn to the living God, because we realize that the fountain of life is not within us. We come to the source of life. No one is totally independent and has the self-reliance to meet every situation alone. Jesus Christ is the one who said, "If any man thirst, let him come to me and drink." Jesus said to the woman at the well, "If you knew the gift of God and who it is that is saying to you, 'Give me a drink,' you would have asked him, and he would have given you living water" (John 4:10). Christ offers us the water of life that can satisfy our deepest needs. The anguished cry of every person, "I thirst for the living God," is supplied by the living God, not by material things. This longing is quenched, not by a God restricted by the past, but a God actively working in our lives.

The apostle Paul wrote that the church is a household—a family. A community of faith where brothers and sisters support and sustain one another, the church is the household of God. The church is an assembly—*ekklesia*—the people of the living God, whether only two, three, or hundreds, gathered together to receive strength from God and one another in worship together. The Pioneering Church is a church that is the pillar and buttress of truth. It will not be frightened by truth no matter where it is encountered. It remembers that its Lord said, "You will know the truth, and the truth will make you free (John 8:31). It is not frightened by truth from science, technology, or any other arena, because Jesus Christ has made it truly free. It will follow the path of truth wherever it leads. The church will support the truth even if every one else seeks to destroy it.

A pioneering church is always dreaming, always seeking new visions, aware that God goes before it. God constantly goes before us, leading us into deeper truths, deeper ministries, and more profound ways of being Church. John Killinger noted in his book *The Second Coming of the Church* that the church of the future may have new forms, shapes, and modes of ministry that we would not even recognize today. It may not appear to be the same institution. Killinger challenges the church to be open to God who declares that there are no limits to its possibilities.

At times, I have to confess, I become very discouraged as a pastor. Too many of us identify with the false churches and not the Church of the Living God. But on a depressing winter day, I look out my study window and see a large oak tree that is bare of its leaves, void of life at all. If I look at it closely, I will see on each limb tiny, dormant buds waiting to bring life back to the tree. That tree is a living parable. God's church, filled with dormant buds, waits for the springtime of God's breath to breathe new life into it.

Don't surrender your life to The Only Understanding of Truth Church, because Jesus Christ is always breaking through our old wineskins to bring new insights and truth. It cannot contain or hold back the Living God. Don't settle for religion that is primarily entertainment, but be open to a deep, awesome worship of the Eternal God. Don't settle for the traditional, apathetic church when Christ wants to lead you into a living relationship with the God who is alive and at work in the church.

"Attend the church of your choice." Which do you choose? I hope it will be The Church of the Living God.

# The Church
# The Faces of Christ

## *Guy G. Sayles, Jr.*

They devoted themselves to the apostles' teaching and fellowship, to the breaking of bread and the prayers. Awe came upon everyone, because many wonders and signs were being done by the apostles. All who believed were together and had all things in common; they would sell their possessions and goods and distribute the proceeds to all, as any had need. Day by day, as they spent much time together in the temple, they broke bread at home and ate their food with glad and generous hearts, praising God and having the goodwill of all the people. And day by day the Lord added to their number those who were being saved. (Acts 2:42-47)

Let us hold fast to the confession of our hope without wavering, for he who has promised is faithful. And let us consider how to provoke one another to love and good deeds, not neglecting to meet together, as is the habit of some, but encouraging one another, and all the more as you see the Day approaching. (Heb 10:23-25)

## Faces of the Church
## My Story

When I think of the church, faces come to mind. There is the red, round, grinning face of Oscar Gardner. Mr. Gardner was a deacon in the First Baptist Church of Conley, Georgia, and he was a hand-shaking, back-slapping machine. He would circle that sanctuary, welcoming every person who couldn't manage to avoid him. You could hear him all over that cavernous room, booming out his "hello," and guffawing at jokes—usually his own jokes.

There was Mrs. Ruby Hornsby; she had beautiful hair that was about half strawberry red and half silvery-gray, piercing blue eyes, milk-white skin, and a tight little smile that you had to strain to see. Mrs. Hornsby and her husband had been unable to have children, so they sort of adopted me. Since both my father and mother sang in the choir, I sat between the Hornsbys during worship. He would help me find the hymns and share his Bible with me. She would slip me candy during worship, peppermints she had carefully unwrapped before the service began so that she wouldn't rustle the plastic during the pastor's sermon.

There was Mrs. Ellen Hawkins, whom I called "Miss Ellen," though she had been married. She had a hard but somehow kindly face, and hair stacked high on her head in a kind of beehive arrangement, lacquered into place with a healthy supply of a hair spray that smelled to me like nail polish remover. She taught Training Union for adults who had joined our church; and, even though I was what we then called a "junior boy," I got special permission to attend her class. She loved to talk about Baptist history and doctrine, and I loved to hear about it. So, virtually every Sunday night, I would meet with her in a little room upstairs, near the baptistery, which seemed like a good place for a class on Baptist history.

Along with those faces from childhood, there are others that mean church to me. There is the face of Louis Nelson, who had twinkling eyes that contrasted with his usually sober expression. It did not take long for me to learn that the twinkling eyes were the reflection of a glad and generous heart; the sober expression was something he had put on, like a tie, for his job with the Federal Reserve Bank. He and his wife, Loice, were our neighbors in Indiana. Anita and I were seminary students, and I was trying hard to learn what it meant to be a pastor in a real church and not just in the church described in my classes. When he sensed that the tension between my experience and my idealism was growing too great, he would go out on in the back yard, get in his big swing, and wait for me to get home from school. He'd motion me over and ask something like, "Well, what do you have on your mind today?" Then, he'd answer his question, putting my dilemmas into words. I learned a lot about life and church from Louis Nelson, and that backyard class on the nature and purpose of the church was one of the best I ever had.

There is the face of Mack Charles Jones. Mack's was a big and black and loving face; his eyes flashed and wept with a passion for justice. He was the pastor of the First Baptist Church, Fannin Street in LaGrange, Georgia—the major black church in that city. We became fast friends; and, when I would bump into some problem, he would call and say, "Hey man; I just want you to know I'm here." Often, God sounded like Mack Charles Jones to me.

There are the faces of children, who, at every church I have served, have bounced into my office, offering smiles, drawings, and suggestions of books I might want to read. There are teenagers' faces

—some shadowy and sullen with self-doubt and seething rage, some bright with hope and promise—who simply by showing up at all have spoken to me of a yearning they have to make sense of life. There are the tear-stained faces of people who have admitted to things of which they are ashamed and guilty; the joyful faces of people who have asked me to check my calendar to see when I might perform their weddings; and the confused, bewildered faces of seekers after guidance. When I think of church, I see faces.

In those faces, there is Jesus. A bright phrase in one of Gerrard Manley Hopkins' poems has captured my imagination:

> For Christ plays in ten thousand places,
> Lovely in limbs, and lovely in eyes not his
> To the Father through the features of men's faces.[1]

It was Hopkins' belief, and it is mine, that we catch a glimpse of Christ in one another's faces. So it is that Theresa of Calcutta is fond of saying, "Let the Christ in me serve the Christ in you."

Sentiment should not outrun reality, however. Not every face at every moment reminds me of Jesus. There are times when the faces of my sisters and brothers in Christ remind me of almost anything and anyone except Jesus! There are times when my own face signals more frustration and rejection than it does Christ's affirmation and welcome. Still, over time, the people who make up Christ's community have been the channel through which Christ has come to me. The church—filled with faces loving and kind, fragile and flawed—bears the image of Jesus Christ.

# Faces of the Church
# The New Testament Story

The Church exists for the sake of Jesus Christ. We are here to love and serve him; and, as we love and serve Jesus, he turns our attention to one another and to the world. He tells us that we will find him in each other: "Where two or three are gathered in my name, I am there among them" (Matt 18:20). "Just as you did it to one of the least of these who are members of my family, you did it to me" (Matt 25:40). As Simone Weil put it, "Nothing among human things has such power to keep our gaze fixed ever more intently upon God, than friendship for the friends of God."[2] We are here for him. He is here for us. We are here for one another.

Nearly every New Testament snapshot of the church is a group photo. There are very few individual portraits. Look for instance at Acts 2:

> All who believed were together, and they had all things in common; they would sell their possessions and goods and distribute the proceeds to all, as any had need. Day by day, as they spent much time together in the temple, they broke bread at home and ate their food with glad and generous hearts, praising God and having the good will of all the people. And day by day the Lord added to their number those who were being saved. (Acts 2:44-47)

Together, in the meeting of needs. Together, in the worship of God. Together, in the joy of fellowship around the table. That's how the New Testament church looks: a group of people called together *by* Christ to be together *in* Christ.

## Faces of the Church
## The Baptist Story

Our Baptist forebears knew how important the community was to our experience of, and witness for, Jesus Christ. Many of them spoke of the church as a *covenant community*, a fellowship of believers bound to God and one another by promises of mutual faithfulness, by the practice of graceful but real accountability, and by the power of enduring love. At the founding (in 1616) of what became one of the earliest Baptist churches in England, "the Jacob-Lathrop-Jessey Church," the members of that congregation entered into a covenant relationship:

> Standing together, they joined hands, and solemnly covenanted with each other in the presence of Almighty God: To walk together in all God's ways and ordinances, according as he had already revealed, or should further make known to them.[3]

As passionate as our forebears were in their promotion and protection of individual liberty of conscience, they also were keenly aware of the need for such individual liberty to find nurture, expression, and accountability in the community of faith. They insisted on freedom, and they exercised that freedom by willingly binding themselves to the covenant community.

# Faces of the Church
# Our Commitment to Community

Scripture and our Baptist heritage teach us that commitment to Christ involves a commitment to his community. How do you feel about that claim? I can imagine that some of you wish there could be some way to have Christ and have very little to do with the church. In fact, that's how many people approach the church these days. They want to be *in* just far enough to keep Jesus in their sights, but *out* far enough to be out of view when the church comes looking for support and involvement. "Please, just let me slip in and rush out."

I understand that desire, and, of course, you are free to stay on the fringes. I believe our churches should welcome and encourage people without applying "full-court pressure." There are people who come to our churches who are searching, and they're not at all sure about Christianity. There are people who are wounded, and it will take time for them to be able to heal. There are people who are tired and burned out, and they don't see how they can get involved. There are people who are grieving, or who are angry at God; and they are in our churches, hoping against hope, to see light, but so far find themselves stuck in the dark night of the soul. Everyone who feels the need to be on the edge and not in the center should be welcomed.

Many of us resist community, not for those reasons, but because making a *commitment* to a group of people means making a commitment to a group of *people,* and people are so hopelessly human. They have strange ideas and unreasonable expectations. Some have big egos disguised as devoted and sacrificial servants. Some have weak egos masquerading as know-it-alls. Some are Republicans. There are people in church that you'd never spend time with if you had the choice. There are people who listen to Rush Limbaugh, and others to *Fresh Air* on N.P.R. Some are Democrats. There are children, and you've raised yours. There are people who remind you of your mother and father, and you've moved away from yours. To be committed to the church means getting tangled-up with all these people, and who's got the time and energy for that?

Both the New Testament and Christian experiences through the centuries teach us that it is vital for us to find the time and energy for Christian community. Without the church, we are not likely to grow and flourish as followers of Jesus Christ. In ways we may not fully have acknowledged, we need the church.

We need the church, because the church keeps telling the gospel story. Most of us would not have experienced the grace of Jesus Christ had there not been people who cared enough to tell us the story. Those people who showed us and shared with us the gospel were church people, people who were sustained and challenged by the community to demonstrate and declare the love of God revealed in Jesus Christ. The vast majority of us would not be Christian had it not been for the people who make up the church. So it was that theologian Emil Brunner wrote:

> The Ekklesia is always prior to the individual believers; they have become believers through being drawn into it. Every believer has received his [or her] faith through the communications of others. [They] are thus already in a fellowship when [they] become . . . believer[s].[4]

It's not just at the beginning of our faith that we need for the church to tell the story. We need for the church to keep telling the story, because we keep ignoring, forgetting, and confusing the story. Annie Dillard recently said,

> I have no problem with miracles. I'm a long way from agnosticism, and no longer even remember how a lot of things that used to be problems for me were. But that isn't the question I struggle with. To me, the real question is, How in the world can we *remember* God?[5]

Who but the church will recall for us that judgment is not God's last word but that mercy is? Who but the church will keep reminding us that guilt is not final but grace is? Who but the church will keep insisting that life is not a drive for power but a search for ways to serve? That life is not possession but stewardship? That faith overcomes anxiety, love casts out fear, and hope conquers despair? Who but the church will keep telling us God's story, the story in which our lives find meaning and direction? Because we need the gospel story, we need the church.

We need the church, because we need encouragement; we need for members of the community to help us be faithful to that vision of life we have seen in Jesus Christ. We need for them to call us back to our true selves, the Christlike selves we already are and are in the process of becoming. You might prefer the term *accountability*, but I doubt it. Whatever you call it, we need our Christian friends to ask us where we've been, and how it's going, and where we're headed. We need for them to challenge us when they think we've got it all wrong, affirm us when they think we've got it right, and, in either case, assure us of their tender-tough love.

When the renowned British philosopher C. P. Snow died, his friend J. H. Plumb

> wrote of him in an obituary which appeared in the Christ College magazine, "He possessed that great quality of making all whom he met feel larger than life, better scientists, better writers, better historians, indeed better [people]."[6]

We all need people like that in our lives, encouraging us to be better Christians, better human beings; and we find those people in the community of Christ. The writer of Hebrews urged:

> Let us hold fast to the confession of our hope without wavering, for God who has promised is faithful. And let us consider how to provoke one another to love and good deeds, not neglecting to meet together, as is the habit of some, but encouraging one another. (10:23-25)

In the spirit of those words, Dietrich Bonhoeffer, in *Life Together*, affirmed: "The physical presence of other Christians is a source of incomparable joy and strength to the believer."[7] Because we need encouragement, we need the church.

And the church needs us. For reasons I do not fully fathom, Christ is making himself present to the world largely by means of the church. The church is not perfect, because we are in it; but it is life-giving, because Jesus is in it with us. When Christ calls you to himself, he calls you to the church, so that you can be his face to the people in this room and in this world. Amen.

# Notes

[1]Gerrard Manley Hopkins, *Poems and Prose*, introduction by W. H. Gardner (London: Penguin Books, 1953/1963) 51.

[2]Simone Weil, *Waiting for God* (Collins/Fontana Books, 1950) 40.

[3]Champlain Burrage, *The Church Covenant Idea, Its Origins and Development* (Philadelphia: American Baptist Publication Society, 1904) 79.

[4]Emil Brunner, *The Christian Doctrine of the Church, Faith, and the Consummation* (Philadelphia: Westminster, 1960) 26-27.

[5]Philip Yancey, "A Pilgrim's Progress: Annie Dillard's Career as a Spiritual Spy," *Books and Culture* (September/October, 1995) 12.

[6]Anthony Storr, *Churchill's Black Dog, Kafka's Mice, and Other Phenomena of the Human Mind* (New York: Grove Press, 1988) 112.

[7]Dietrich Bonhoeffer, *Life Together* (New York: Harper & Row, 1954) 19.

# Whose Church Is This, Anyway?

## Walter B. Shurden

So then, remember that at one time you Gentiles by birth, called "the uncircumcision" by those who are called "the circumcision"—a physical circumcision made in the flesh by human hands—remember that you were at that time without Christ, being aliens from the commonwealth of Israel, and strangers to the covenants of promise, having no hope and without God in the world. But now in Christ Jesus you who once were far off have been brought near by the blood of Christ. For he is our peace; in his flesh he has made both groups into one and has broken down the dividing wall, that is, the hostility between us. He has abolished the law with its commandments and ordinances, that he might create in himself one new humanity in place of the two, thus making peace, and might reconcile both groups to God in one body through the cross, thus putting to death that hostility through it. So he came and proclaimed peace to you who were far off and peace to those who were near; for through him both of us have access in one Spirit to the Father. So then you are no longer strangers and aliens, but you are citizens with the saints and also members of the house hold of God, built upon the foundation of the apostles and prophets, with Christ Jesus himself as the cornerstone. In him the whole structure is joined together and grows into a holy temple in the Lord; in whom you also are built together spiritually into a dwelling place for God.

This is the reason that I Paul am a prisoner for Christ Jesus for the sake of you Gentiles—for surely you have already heard of the commission of God's grace that was given me for you, and how the mystery was made known to me by revelation, as I wrote above in a few words, a reading of which will enable you to perceive my understanding of the mystery of Christ. In former generations this mystery was not made known to humankind, as it has now been revealed to his holy apostles and prophets by the Spirit: that is, the Gentiles have become fellow heirs, members of the same body, and sharers in the promise in Christ Jesus through the gospel.

Of this gospel I have become a servant according to the gift of God's grace that was given me by the working of his power. Although I am the very least of all the saints, this grace was given to me to bring to the Gentiles the news of the boundless riches of Christ, and to make everyone see what is the plan of the mystery hidden for ages in God who created all things; so that through the church the wisdom of God in its rich variety might now be made known to the rulers and authorities in the heavenly places. This was in accordance with the eternal purpose that he has carried out in Christ Jesus our Lord, in whom we have access to God in boldness and confidence through faith in him. I pray, therefore that you may not lose heart over my sufferings for you; they are your glory. (Eph 2:11–3:13)

*[This sermon, with some slight revisions, was preached at the historic First Baptist Church in Greenville, South Carolina, on August 23, 1992, at the launching of a campaign to complete a building program for the church. References are made in the sermon to the church, its heritage, and its commitment to future ministry.]*

*****

Twenty-nine years-old and straight out of my graduate work in seminary, I was being interviewed by the pulpit search committee of the First Baptist Church in Ruston, Louisiana. Fred Jones, the city judge, chaired the committee. Things went well; we liked them, and they seemed to like us. So they invited us to visit the town and see the church facilities.

Upon getting out of the car at the church building, Fred intoned in his most solemn and judge-like voice, "Walter, you *will* get negative votes when the committee presents you to the church as pastor." I thought to myself, "Thanks, Fred, aren't you an encouraging little helper." Then he added immediately, "But don't take the votes personally; they will be votes against me as chair of the search committee." Then he said, "Some people in Ruston contend that I think that the initials FBC in First Baptist Church really stand for 'Fred's Baptist Church.' "

Fred Jones, and a handful of other lay people, launched me in ministry in more ways than I can say grace over. One thing in particular Fred did with his diabolical humor on that particular day was to engage me with the question: "Whose Church Is This?"

How do you answer? How do you answer about this old historic and heritage-laden First Baptist Church of Greenville, South Carolina? Whose church is *this*? What do you say to that question? What say the Scriptures to that question?

# Whose Church Is This?
# This Is the Church of Jesus Christ

This is the only place to begin in answering the question. The heritage of this church reaches much further back than 1823 when William B. Johnson (later the first president of the Southern Baptist Convention) came here and began "preaching in the courthouse . . . and solicited funds on the streets to build a Baptist meeting house."[1]

You folks have a heritage that reaches back further than that. This is God's church! Here is the first answer to the question, "Whose church is this?" It is first not only in chronological order, but also in primary importance. Every other answer is secondary and subordinate.

This is not first and foremost a denominational church. This is not first of all a South Carolina church or a Greenville church or a Baptist church. This is certainly not an elitist church. This is not even "your" church, those of you who give your money and energy and gifts to this fellowship. This is God's church! This we really need to get straight, don't we?

Not once but twice Paul said it in our text for today: "You are no longer strangers and aliens, but you are . . . members of the household *of God*" (Eph 2:19). And again, "You . . . are . . . a dwellingplace *for God*" (2:22). The "church," whatever its sectarian label and wherever its location, is first of all owned by God.

Fred's critics were right. It was not "Fred's Baptist Church." It is never primarily "my" church or "our" church or "your" church. It is foundationally and fundamentally *God's church*. If you ask the question, "Whose church is this?" and frame your response in terms of ownership, the answer is clear. It is God's church. This is the church of God, the church of Christ.

The church of God is part of what is meant by the word *oikoumene*, the universal church of Christ. This fact speaks to what First Baptist Church, Greenville, South Carolina, has in common with all God's people—all Christians everywhere.

Your worship here reflects your identification with the larger body of Christ. Your policies affirm your affectionate link with Christians of other traditions. Some of us who were reared Baptists have been embarrassed most of our lives by the sectarian and narrow spirit that often marked our denominational tradition. I heard of a sign in front of a church that read: "This is the only church authorized by God to represent Christ on earth!" Too many of us heard too much that sounded too close to that as we grew up in some Baptist communities. It is time to shake that tradition once and for all.

As you read Loulie O. Pettigrew's history of this church, you realize that such narrowness has never been part of your local church tradition. Your children will one day rise and up and call you blessed because you gave them in this place a large view of the meaning of church. You have sought to teach them the historic Baptist heritage, but you have gone beyond that. You have said by word and deed that God's church is bigger than this church, bigger than all Baptist churches put together. That is not only what our Bible says. That is also what our best Baptist heritage says. Christ's church is bigger than this church.

## Whose Church Is This? This Is "Their" Church

This is the church of all those who have come before you. I've read your church's history, and it is a good one. Incidentally, reading one's local church history ought to be an annual requirement of every church member everywhere. And that despite the fact that local histories are often dreadfully researched, appallingly organized, and boringly written, all of which testify to the fact that we don't invest adequate money in keeping the story alive and vital at the local church level. Many of us know more about the church generally than we do our own churches specifically. Gratitude grows better in local gardens. Most of you know the names of Augustine, Martin Luther, John Calvin, and John Wesley.

May I tell you whose church this is? This is the church of James Hyde, Elizabeth D. Sloan, Elizabeth Ligon, Emma McGregor, Sarah Cleveland, Dinah Hyde, Frances Rhodes, Elizabeth Rhodes, Emmala E. Thompson and Mahala Fleming. Count them! Nine women and one man! It is a fact that there would not be many Baptist churches had the women boycotted! This is the church of "those ten." "Those ten people"—names many of you doubtless do not recognize but to whom you are deeply indebted—constituted this church on November 2, 1831. "Those ten people"—that is whose church this is.

One way to respond to the question, "Whose church is this?" is to answer in terms of its historical identity. Paul wrote to the Ephesians and to us, reminding them and us that we are "fellow citizens with the saints and members of the household of God, *built upon the foundation* of the apostles and prophets" (Eph 2:19-20).

Those of us here today entered the parade late. We were late-comers to the great *ekklesia*; most of you who are members here came late to this particular *ekklesia*. We are heirs. We are beneficiaries. We are the lucky ones! We stand on the shoulders of those who helped to ignite the spark and keep the fire going. And then others came along and fanned the flame with confessions of faith and commitments of lives and investments of dollars and dimes.

Whose church is this? This is the church of "those ten people" who started the ball rolling 161 years ago. Whose church? Why this is the church of Samuel Gibson and Sanford Vandiver who were the first pastors, each preaching once a month. And this is the church of A. M. Spalding, the church's first full-time minister, and it is the church of Gabriel Poole, a black man licensed to preach by this church in 1847. This is the church of all those who from 1831 have invested, not only their money, but their very lives in this fellowship.

If you have visited the First Baptist Church in Nashville, Tennessee, you know that they have a beautiful and relatively new sanctuary. When they built the new sanctuary, Franklin Paschall, their pastor, urged them to retain the tower of the old church building and attach the new sanctuary to it. That is exactly what the congregation did. That old tower attached to that new sanctuary is an architectural reminder that First Baptist Church in Nashville is "their" church, the church of all those who went before in another day and time. We really do need to keep "pieces of the past" as reminders to us about whose church this is, don't we?

Roman Catholics and some others may make too much of All Saints' Day, but we Baptists make too little of those who passed us the baton of faith. First Baptist Church, Greenville, is a memorial church, just as is every other local Christian church. It is a memorial first to Christ who loved us and gave himself for us, and second to those who followed in his steps and gave themselves sacrificially to continue the ministry of this church over these years. As you begin a most important stewardship campaign today, and—in the words of your slogan—to "claim a new name," and launch a new era in the life of your church, don't forget to be thankful for all those who handed you the pen and the opportunity to write a new chapter.

# Whose Church Is This?
# This Is Your Church!

If you answer in terms of ownership, this is *God's* Church! It is Christ's church. If you answer in terms of historical identity, this is *their* church! It belongs to all those who bequeathed it to you. But if you answer in terms of contemporary stewardship, this is *your* church! "No longer strangers and aliens," Paul said. Now we are "fellow citizens," "members." Once far off, we've been brought into the fold. You belong. This is YOUR church!

In a very real sense, First Baptist Church of Ruston, Louisiana, was Fred's Baptist Church. Not his by himself, but his in fellowship with all those other priests of God at 200 South Trenton.

And this is *your* church. *Your* church, but not in the sense of a private club. One does not have to have a pass key to enter these doors to worship and learn. It is not "yours" in that kind of private or possessive sense.

But in another sense—in the sense of duty and responsibility and stewardship—this is surely *your* church. In this case the pronoun is plural not singular. It is "our" church, not "my" church. It speaks of community, not individualism; togetherness not personal property.

"Our" church. That phrase speaks to the way you do your business and govern yourselves. It speaks to the Baptist emphasis of congregational church government. Baptists do not have bishop church government or pastor church government. It is not government by a handful, but government by a churchfull. You—the membership—of this church vote to approve the church's budget, design the church's ministry, and execute the church's task. You are all priests before God.

I once heard the chair of a search committee give a flowery introduction for the new pastor on the pastor's first Sunday at the church. The closing line of the introduction: "Now, we want to all do what we can and support the pastor in his ministry among us and to the community." Theologically, biblically, and baptistically, it was a wrong line. It is not "his ministry" or "her ministry." It is "our" ministry.

One of the most laughable dimensions of the controversy among Southern Baptists in the 1980s was the flap about the authority of the pastor. One prominent fundamentalist pastor said that the pastor was the "ruler of the church." He pastors a different kind of Baptist church from any I have ever pastored or been a member of or ever want to be a member of.

Pastoral leadership? Of course! Respect for the ministry? Why, yes, of course! Pastoral voice in terms of the direction of the church? Surely. But pastor as "ruler" or "final word" or "dominating personality" in the church? Of course not!

This is *your* church.

*Yours* the responsibility to pass on to the next generation what has been so graciously bequeathed to you. You pledge your money to this church, not simply for yourself, but in the name of your children, your grandchildren, your grandmothers, and your grandfathers.

It is *YOUR* church!

Yours the stewardship.

Yours the governance.

Yours the bills to pay.

Yours the ministry of Christ to embrace.

John Sutherland Bonnell was the longtime pastor of the historic Fifth Avenue Presbyterian Church in New York City. He was called rather suddenly to visit a man who had suffered his first heart attack. The patient had been placed in one of those old oxygen tents to ease the stress on his heart. Understandably, the person was frightened by the tent and all that it suggested. Standing beside his bed, at an appropriate moment, Dr. Bonnell zipped down the side of the oxygen tent, put his head inside and spoke calmly to his friend, "Now that we are both inside this tent together, let's breathe this air together."

That's the spirit of commitment in a local church. This particular congregation is *your* tent. You breathe the air of life and heritage and grace and accountability together.

Whose church is this? If you respond to that question in terms of the daily function of the church, the answer is clear: the church belongs to the entire priesthood of believers operating on an equal footing in this particular place.

## Whose Church Is This?
## This Is the "World's" Church

In terms of ownership, it is God's church. In terms of historical identity, it is "theirs," all of those who have gone before you in this place. In terms of stewardship and responsibility, it is "your" church.

There is yet one more very important way to answer the question. In terms of mission and purpose, this church belongs to the whole human race.

Paul never tired of saying it. He called it the great "mystery of Christ" (Eph 3:4). *Everybody* is included in the community of faith. In a very literal sense, Paul "opened" the doors of the church to us all, Gentiles as well as Jews.

One of the first theological books to make an impact on my infant faith was a commentary on the book in the Bible known as Acts. Frank Stagg, one of the three or four greatest teachers I ever had, wrote the book. The thesis of Stagg's book is that the church belongs to all the people of the world.

Stagg points out that the early Christians, most of whom were Jews, wanted to keep the gospel restricted to their kind, to those who observed the laws of Judaism. But in the book of Acts, Luke presents a gospel that is "unhindered." It literally bursts out of religious and racial and geographical prejudices. Acts shows the early Christians' hard-fought struggle to create an inclusive community.

The early church in Acts moved from a narrow Palestinian Jewish sect to include Hellenistic Jews (Acts 6:1-6). And then the church embraced Samaritans or half-Jews with this "unhindered" gospel (Acts 8:1-14). Next, God-fearing Gentiles, like the Ethiopian eunuch (Acts 8:26-40) and Cornelius (Acts 10:1-48), students of Judaism, found an open door to God through Christ. Finally, says Stagg, Gentiles with no relationship to Judaism whatsoever, people like the Philippian jailor (Acts 16:25-34), discovered that "whosoever will may come."

The "unhindered gospel." Here is a truth we must bring ourselves back to Sunday after Sunday: a local church is not intended to be a catch basin; it is a conduit. Our task in our local church fellowships is not simply to create mental health for our families and ourselves. The bricks of these buildings are put here in the name of Christ. They are not here exclusively for us to enjoy. Some churches, I have noticed, use their facilities as if they were a private club, for the membership and no one else. The programs of this church are not designed simply for an "in" group.

Every local congregation of believers must monitor itself lest it become motivated by self-interest. If we are not careful at the local church level, we will be building bigger and better barns—for ourselves! I am sure that Carlyle Marney was right about many things, but I am positive he hit the bull's eye on this one: when a church answers the question "Whose church is this?" in terms of mission to the hurting ones of the world, every other church question is easy to handle.

The only serious budget question becomes not "How much will this cost?" or "Are we able to raise this much money?" but "Will this help serve the world for whom Christ died?"

The only serious curriculum question is not "Who published this?" or "Where did this material come from?" but "Will this make the truth of the love and mercy of Christ plainer?"

The only important long-range planning question is not "Is this too much for us to shoot for?" but "Does this put us in a position to bless somebody down the road?"

I like your logo for your stewardship campaign. It is a picture of your church spire set against the backdrop of a globe of the world. Can you commit yourself to that vision today? The best definition of church I ever heard was "All who love Christ in the service of all who suffer." All who love Christ . . . in the service of all who suffer.

This is God's church. And this is "their" church. And this is "your" church. But, my friends, since 1831, the mission and purpose of this local body of believers has been to make a difference in God's creation. I would suggest to you that both your building campaign and your "faith fund" can make a real and genuine and authentic difference in the world that God and your predecessors have given you. Our money matters for Christ, doesn't it?

Some time back I was taking another run at this particular sermon in a little country church in Georgia. I kept repeating the question "Whose church is this?" the same way I've done this morning. Tiring of my public ignorance, a little eight-year-old boy leaned over to his mother and said out loud, "Mamma, somebody needs to tell that man whose church this is."

Honestly, I think I know whose church this is. Do you? Do you know whose this church this is? So, what now?

# Note

[1]Loulie O. Pettigrew, "First Baptist Church Heritage: Beginnings," *The News*, 10 June 1992.

# The Baptist Doctrine of the Church

*[Editor's Note: The Council of the Baptist Union of Great Britain and Ireland approved this marvelous exposition of the Baptist vision of the church in 1948. An extraordinarily lucid document, it is an effort on the part of Baptists in England and Ireland to describe their view of the church in the mid-twentieth century, and it deserves serious consideration by Baptists around the world at the end of the twentieth century. Baptists of England have contributed to the larger Baptist movement far out of proportion to their present relatively small numbers. Any effort to understand the Baptist vision of the church should take seriously any pronouncement from that country. Some Baptists in the United States, especially those influenced by Landmarkism and Fundamentalism, will find some rather unfamiliar notes struck in this document.*

*First, the recurring themes of freedom and liberty are found throughout the document. Second, a firm ecumenical note is sounded while Baptist distinctives are maintained. In fact, the first article in the document is that of "The One Holy Catholic Church." Third, worship, while guided by "spontaneity and freedom," is to be characterized by "disciplined preparation of every part of the service." Fourth, the ministry, although an exalted office, is a ministry of "a church and not only a ministry of an individual." All ministerial authority comes from Christ and "through the believing community." Fifth, believer's baptism and the Lord's Supper are portrayed as "sacraments" that are "means of grace."*

*The source for this document is Ernest A. Payne, The Baptist Union: A Short History (London: Carey Kingsgate Press Ltd., 1958) 283-91. In the original document the notes were at the bottom of the pages. These notes have been inserted into the text, but the bibliography has been retained as in the original document. Also, the British style of spelling, punctuation, and capitalization is retained.]*

## "The Baptist Doctrine of the Church"

1. The Baptist Union of Great Britain and Ireland represents more than three thousand churches and about three hundred thousand members. Through its membership in the Baptist World Alliance it is in fellowship with other Baptist communities through the world numbering about thirteen million, who have accepted the responsibilities of full communicant membership.

Baptists have a continuous history in Great Britain since the beginning of the seventeenth century. Many of their principles, however, were explicitly proclaimed in the second half of the sixteenth century by the radical wing of the Reformation movement. They claim as their heritage also the great central stream of Christian doctrine and piety through the centuries, and have continuity with the New Testament Church in that they rejoice to believe and seek faithfully to proclaim the Apostolic Gospel and endeavour to build up the life of their churches after what seems to them the New Testament pattern.

## The One Holy Catholic Church

2. Although Baptists have for so long held a position separate from that of other communions, they have always claimed to be part of the one holy catholic Church of our Lord Jesus Christ. They believe in the catholic Church as the holy society of believers in our Lord Jesus Christ, which He founded, of which He is the only Head, and in which He dwells by His Spirit, so that though manifested in many communions, organized in various modes, and scattered throughout the world, it is yet one in Him (See "The Baptist Reply to the Lambeth Appeal"). The Church is the Body of Christ and a chosen instrument of the divine purpose in history.

In the worship, fellowship and witness of the one Church we know ourselves to be united in the communion of saints, not only with all believers upon earth, but also with those who have entered into life everlasting.

The origin of the Church is in the Gospel—in the mighty acts of God, the Incarnation, Ministry, Death, Resurrection and Ascension of our Lord and the Descent of the Holy Spirit. Thus it is the power of God in Christ which created the Church and which sustains it through the centuries. It is historically significant that Christ, at the outset of His ministry, "chose twelve to be with Him" and gathered His people into a new community. In our judgment there is no evidence in the New Testament to show that He formally organized the Church, but He did create it. This "New Israel", the expansion of which is recorded in the Acts of the Apostles and the Epistles, is the heir to the "Old Israel", yet it is marked by vital and significant differences. It is based upon the New Covenant; membership is not constituted by racial origins but by a personal allegiance; the ritual of temple and synagogue has given place to the ordinances of the Gospel and the national consciousness has widened to world horizons. The Messianic community was reborn by the events of the Gospel and is "a new creation". Therefore, whilst there is an historical continuity with the Old Israel, Old Testament analogies do not determine the character and structure of the New Testament Church.

## The Structure of Local Baptist Churches

3. (a) It is in membership of a local church in one place that the fellowship of the one holy catholic Church becomes significant. Indeed, such gathered companies of believers are the local manifestation of the one Church of God on earth and in heaven. Thus the church at Ephesus is described, in words which strictly belong to the whole catholic Church, as "the church of God, which He hath purchased with His own blood" (Acts xx.28). The vital relationship to Christ which is implied in full communicant membership in a local church carries with it membership in the Church which is both in time and in eternity, both militant and triumphant. To worship and serve in such a local Christian community is, for Baptists, of the essence of Churchmanship.

Such churches are gathered by the will of Christ and live by the indwelling of His Spirit. They do not have their origin, primarily, in human resolution. Thus the Baptist Confession of 1677 (McGlothlin, 265) which deals at length with doctrine and church order, uses phrases which indicate that local churches are formed by the response of believers to the Lord's command. Out of many such phrases we may quote the following: "Therefore they do willingly consent to walk together according to the appointment of Christ." Churches are gathered "according to His mind, declared in His word". Membership was not regarded as a private option, for the CONFESSION continues: "All believers are bound to join themselves to particular churches when and where they have opportunity so to do." In our tradition discipleship involves both church membership and a full acceptance of the idea of churchmanship.

(b) The basis of our membership in the church is a conscious and deliberate acceptance of Christ as Saviour and Lord by each individual. There is, we hold, a personal crisis in the soul's life when a person stands alone in God's presence, responds to God's gracious activity, accepts His forgiveness and commits to the Christian way of life. Such a crisis may be swift and emotional or slow-developing and undramatic, and is normally experienced within and because of our life in the Christian community, but it is always a personal experience wherein God offers His salvation in Christ, and the individual, responding by faith, receives the assurance of the Spirit that by grace he or she is the child of God. It is this vital evangelical experience which underlies the Baptist conception of the Church and is both expressed and safeguarded by the sacrament of Believers' Baptism.

(c) The life of a gathered Baptist church centres in worship, in the preaching of the Word, in the observance of the two sacraments of Believers' Baptism and the Lord's Supper, in growth in fellowship and in witness and service to the world outside. Our forms of worship are in the Reformed tradition and are not generally regulated by liturgical forms. Our tradition is one of spontaneity and freedom, but we hold that there should be disciplined preparation of every part of the service. The sermon, as an exposition of the Word of God and a means of building up the faith and life of the congregation, has a central place in public worship. The scriptures are held by us to be the primary authority both for the individual in his or her belief and way of life and for the Church in its teaching and modes of government. It is the objective revelation given in scripture which is the safeguard against a purely subjective authority in religion. We firmly hold that each must search the scriptures for himself or herself and seek the illumination of the Holy Spirit to interpret them. We know also that Church history and Christian experience through the centuries are a guide to the meaning of scripture. Above all, we hold that the eternal Gospel—the life, death and resurrection of our Lord—is the fixed point from which our interpretation, both of the Old and New Testaments, and of later developments in the Church, must proceed.

The worship, preaching, sacramental observances, fellowship and witness are all congregational acts of the whole church in which each member shares responsibility, for all are held to be of equal standing in Christ, though there is a diversity of gifts and a difference of functions. This responsibility and this equality are focused in the church meeting which, under Christ, cares for the well-being of the believing community and appoints its officers. It is the responsibility of each member, according to one's gifts, to build up the life of sisters and brothers and to maintain the spiritual health of the church (Rom xv.14). It is the church meeting which takes the responsibility of exercising that discipline whereby the church withdraws from members who are unruly and have ceased to share in its convictions and life.

The church meeting, though outwardly a democratic way of ordering the affairs of the church, has deeper significance. It is the occasion when, as individuals and as a community, we submit ourselves to the guidance of the Holy Spirit and stand under the judgments of God that we may know what is the mind of Christ. We believe that the structure of local churches just described springs from the Gospel and best preserves its essential features.

(d) The Christian doctrine of the Trinity asserts a relationship of Persons within the Godhead, and God has revealed Himself in the Person of His Son, our Saviour Jesus Christ. Thus the Gospel is the basis of the Christian evaluation of men and women as persons. Behind the idea of the gathered church lies the profound conviction of the importance of each Christian's growth to spiritual maturity and of the responsibility which, as a member of the divine family, she or he should constantly exercise.

(e) Although each local church is held to be competent, under Christ, to rule its own life, Baptists, throughout their history, have been aware of the perils of isolation and have sought safeguards against exaggerated individualism. From the seventeenth century there have been "Associations" of Baptist churches which sometimes appointed Messengers; more recently, their fellowship with one another has been greatly strengthened by the Baptist Union, the Baptist Missionary Society and the Baptist World Alliance. In recent years, General Superintendents have been appointed by the Baptist Union to have the care of churches in different areas. Indeed, we believe that a local church lacks one of the marks of a truly Christian community if it does not seek the fellowship of other Baptist churches, does not seek a true relationship with Christians and churches of other communions and is not conscious of its place in the one catholic Church. To quote again from the Confession of 1677: "As each church and all the members of it are bound to pray continually for the good and prosperity of all the churches of Christ in all places; and upon occasions to further it . . . so the churches . . . out to hold communion amongst themselves for their peace, increase of love and mutual edification."

## The Ministry

4. A properly ordered Baptist church will have its duly appointed officers. These will include the minister (or pastor), elders, deacons, Sunday school teachers and other church workers. The Baptist conception of the ministry is governed by the principle that it is a ministry of a church and not only a ministry of an individual. It is the church which preaches the Word and celebrates the sacraments, and it is the church which, through pastoral oversight, feeds the flock and ministers to the world. It normally does these things through the

person of its minister, but not solely through the minister. Any member of the church may be authorized by it, on occasion, to exercise the functions of the ministry, in accordance with the principle of the priesthood of all believers, to preach the Word, to administer baptism, to preside at the Lord's table, to visit, and comfort or rebuke members of the fellowship.

Baptists, however, have had from the beginning an exalted conception of the office of the Christian minister and have taken care to call their pastors. The minister's authority to exercise the ministerial office comes from the call of God in personal experience, but this call is tested and approved by the church of which the minister is a member and (as is increasingly the rule) by the representatives of a large group of churches. Ministers receive intellectual and spiritual training and are then invited to exercise their gifts in a particular sphere. Ministerial authority, therefore, is from Christ through the believing community. It is not derived from a chain of bishops held to be lineally descended from the Apostles, and we gratefully affirm that to our non-episcopal communities, as to those episcopally governed, the gifts of the Spirit and the power of God are freely given.

Many among us hold that since the ministry is the gift of God to the Church and the call to exercise the functions of a minister comes from Him, a person who is so called is not only the minister of a local Baptist church but also a minister of the whole Church of Jesus Christ.

Ordination takes place when a person has satisfactorily completed college training and has been called to the pastorate of a local church, appointed to chaplaincy service or accepted for service abroad by the Committee of the Baptist Missionary Society. The ordination service is presided over by either the Principal of the college, a General Superintendent or a senior minister and is shared in by other ministers and lay representatives of the church. Though there is no prescribed or set form of service, it invariably includes either a personal statement of faith or answers to a series of questions regarding the faith. From the seventeenth century onwards, ordination took place with the laying on of hands: in the nineteenth century this custom fell into disuse, but is now again increasingly practised.

## The Sacraments

5. In the preceding sections we have sought to describe the life and ministry of Baptist churches. It is in their total activity of worship and

prayer, sacrament and service that the grace of God is continuously given to believing men and women.

We recognize the two sacraments of Believers' Baptism and the Lord's Supper as being of the Lord's ordaining. We hold that both are "means of grace" to those who receive them in faith, and that Christ is really and truly present, not in the material elements, but in the heart and mind and soul of the believer and in the Christian community which observes the sacrament. Our confidence in this rests upon the promises of Christ and not upon any power bestowed on the celebrant in virtue of ordination or succession in ministry. We believe it is important not to isolate the sacraments from the context of the total activity of the worshipping, believing and serving fellowship of the church.

Following the guidance of the New Testament we administer Baptism only to those who have made a responsible and credible profession of "repentance towards God and faith in the Lord Jesus Christ". Such persons are then immersed in the name of the Father, the Son and the Holy Spirit. Salvation is the work of God in Christ, which becomes operative when it is accepted in faith. Thus we do not baptize infants. There is, however, a practice in our churches of presenting young children at a service of public worship where the responsibilities of the parents and the church are recognized and prayers are offered for the parents and the child. Baptists believe that from birth all children are within the love and care of the heavenly Father and therefore within the operation of the saving grace of Christ; hence they have never been troubled by the distinction between baptized and unbaptized children. They have had a notable share with other groups of Christian people in service to children in Sunday schools, orphanages, education and child welfare.

We would claim that the baptism of believers by immersion is in accordance with and sets forth the central facts of the Gospel. It is an "acted creed". We value the symbolism of immersion following the Pauline teaching of the believer's participation in the death, burial and resurrection of our Lord (Romans vi.3). As a matter of history, however, the recovery of the truth that baptism is only for believers preceded by some years the return by Baptists to the primitive mode of baptizing by immersion, and it is a credible and responsible profession of faith on the part of the candidate for baptism which we hold to be essential to the rite. As a means of grace to the believer and to the church and as an act of obedience to our Lord's command, we treasure this sacrament. The New Testament clearly indicates a connection of the gift of the Holy Spirit with the experience of baptism which, without making the rite the necessary or inevitable channel of that gift, yet makes it the appropriate occasion of a new and deeper reception of it.

The Lord's Supper is celebrated regularly in our churches. The form of service, which is "congregational" and in which laypeople have a part, preserves the New Testament conception of the Supper as an act of fellowship, a community meal. Yet as baptism is more than a dramatic representation of the facts of our redemption, so the Communion Service is more than a commemoration of the last Supper and a showing forth "of the Lord's death until He come". Here the grace of God is offered and is received in faith; here the real presence of Christ is manifest in the joy and peace both of the believing soul and of the community; here we are in communion, not only with members in our church, not only with the Church militant on earth and triumphant in heaven, but also with our risen and glorified Lord.

Membership of our local churches is normally consequent on Believers' Baptism, but differences of outlook and practice exist amongst us. "Close Membership" Baptist churches receive into their membership only those who have professed their faith in Christ by passing through the waters of baptism: "Open Membership" churches, though they consist, in the main, of baptized believers, receive also those Christians who profess such faith otherwise than in Believers' Baptism.

Similar differences are to be found amongst us on the question of those who may partake of the Lord's Supper. "Close Communion" churches invite to the Lord's table only those baptized on profession of faith. "Open Communion" churches welcome to the service all "who love the Lord Jesus Christ in sincerity". These differences do not prevent churches of different types from being in communion one with another nor from co-operating in the work of the Baptist Union, the Baptist Missionary Society and the Baptist World Alliance. They are united in the conviction that, in New Testament teaching, personal faith in Christ is essential to the sacraments of the Gospel and the membership of the Church.

## Church and State

6. Our conviction of Christ's Lordship over His church leads us to insist that churches formed by His will must be free from all other

rule in matters relating to their spiritual life. Any form of control by the State in these matters appears to us to challenge the "Crown Rights of the Redeemer". We also hold that this freedom in Christ implies the right of the church to exercise responsible self-government. This has been the Baptist position since the seventeenth century, and it appears to us that the growth of the omnicompetent state and the threat to liberty which has appeared in many parts of the world today make more than ever necessary this witness to spiritual freedom and responsibility which has always been characteristic of the Baptist movement.

This freedom, however, has not led to irresponsibility in our duties as citizens. We believe it is a Christian obligation to honour and serve the State and to labour for the well-being of all men and women. Baptists have shared in many working-class movements, have a not undistinguished record in social service, and were pioneers in the modern missionary movement. They hold that there is a responsibility laid upon each member of the church and upon the churches themselves to apply their faith to all the perplexities of contemporary life.

It will be seen that in this statement of the doctrine of the Church the emphasis falls time and again upon the central fact of evangelical experience, that when God offers His forgiveness, love and power the gift must be personally accepted in faith by each individual. From this follows the believer's endeavour to walk in the way of the Lord and to be obedient to His commandments. From this follows, also, our traditional defence of civil and religious liberty. It governs our conception of the Church and our teaching on Believers' Baptism. Gratefully recognizing the gifts bestowed by God upon other communions, we offer these insights which He has entrusted to us for the service of His whole Church.

# Bibliography

Carver, W. O. "Baptist Churches." *The Nature of the Church*. A Report of the American Theological Committee 1945, of the Continuation Committee, World Conference on Faith and Order.

Cook, Henry. *What Baptists Stand For*. Kingsgate Press, 1947.

Dakin, Arthur. *The Baptist View of the Church and Ministry*. Kingsgate Press, 1944.

Evans, P. W. *Sacraments in the New Testament*. Tyndale Press, 1947.

McGlothlin, W. J. *Baptist Confessions of Faith*. Baptist Historical Society, 1911.

Payne, E. A. *The Fellowship of Believers: Baptist Thought and Practice Yesterday and Today*. Kingsgate Press, 1944 (reprints part of the 1677 Confession of the Particular Baptists and the Reply to the Lambeth Appeal).

———*The Baptist Movement in the Reformation and Onwards*. Kingsgate Press, 1947.

Report of a special committee set up by the Baptist Union on the question of union between Baptists, Congregationalists, and Presbyterians, 1937.

Robinson, H. Wheeler. *Baptist Principles*. Kingsgate Press, 3d edition, 1938.

———*The Life and Faith of the Baptists*. revised edition, Kingsgate Press, 1946.

*The Baptist Position*. A statement prepared by the commission on Baptist principles and policy for study and discussion within the Baptist Convention of Ontario and Quebec, 1947.

"The Baptist Reply to the Lambeth Appeal." Adopted by the Baptist Union Assembly, 4 May 1926. Reprinted by G. K. A. Bell, *Documents on Christian Union*, second series, 102ff.

Underwood, A. C. *A History of English Baptists*. Kingsgate Press, 1947.

Walton, Robert C. *The Gathered Community*. Carey Press, 1946.

Whitley, W. T. *History of British Baptists*. Kingsgate Press, 2d edition, 1932.

# Biographical Notes

**Lavonn D. Brown** is pastor of the First Baptist Church of Norman, Oklahoma, and moderator-elect of the Cooperative Baptist Fellowship.

**Daniel Carro** is pastor of Ramos Mejia Baptist Church and professor at the International Baptist Theological Seminary in Buenos Aires, Argentina.

**Brad Creed** is dean of the George W. Truett Theological Seminary in Waco, Texas.

**Margaret B. Hess** is pastor of the First Baptist Church in Nashua, New Hampshire.

**H. Leon McBeth** is Distinguished Professor of Church History at the Southwestern Baptist Theological Seminary in Fort Worth, Texas.

**Alan Neely** is Henry W. Luce Professor of Ecumenics and Mission, Princeton Theological Seminary, Princeton, New Jersey.

**William R. O'Brien** is director of the Global Center at Beeson Divinity School, Samford University, in Birmingham, Alabama.

**Howard W. Roberts** is senior minister of the First Baptist Church in Auburn, Alabama.

**Guy G. Sayles, Jr.** is pastor of the Woodlands Baptist Church in San Antonio, Texas.

**Walter B. Shurden** is editor of the series *Proclaiming the Baptist Vision* and Callaway Professor and Chair, Department of Christianity, Mercer University, Macon, Georgia.

**Wallace Charles Smith** is senior minister of the Shiloh Baptist Church of Washington, D.C.

**William Powell Tuck** is pastor of the First Baptist Church in Lumberton, North Carolina.

**John R. Tyler,** a layman, is regional manager, network planning for Southwestern Bell Telephone in St. Louis, Missouri.

**Daniel Vestal** is pastor of the Tallowood Baptist Church in Houston, Texas, and first moderator of the Cooperative Baptist Fellowship.